a. m. El...

Oct 5, 1978

THE
BRITISH
ECCENTRIC

THE BRITISH ECCENTRIC

Harriet Bridgeman and
Elizabeth Drury

Clarkson N. Potter, Inc./Publisher NEW YORK

DISTRIBUTED BY CROWN PUBLISHERS, INC.

First American edition published in 1976
by Clarkson N. Potter, Inc.

First published in Great Britain, 1975

Printed in the United States of America

Library of Congress Cataloging in Publication Data
Main Entry under title:

The British eccentric.

1. Eccentrics and eccentricities. 2. Great
Britain—Biography. I. Bridgeman, Harriet.
II. Drury, Elizabeth.
CT9990.B73   1976   920'.041   75-41406
ISBN 0-517-52499-6

Contents

Acknowledgements

Lord Berners: Collins; The Raymond Mander and Joe Mitchenson Theatre Collection; Lord Rossmore; Shell; Robert Heber-Percy, Esq.; The Tatler.

Caraboo: Trustees of the British Museum, London; National Monuments Record, London; David Stockman.

Aleisteir Crowley: Radio Times Hulton Picture Library; The London Library.

The Earl Bishop of Derry: Country Life; The National Trust, Ickworth; Trustees of the British Museum, London; O. G. Jarman; R. B. Fleming.

Sir George Sitwell: Radio Times Hulton Picture Library; Reresby Sitwell, Esq.; Cooper-Bridgeman Library.

Mary Kingsley: The Mansell Collection; 'Travels in West Africa' by Mary Kingsley, Macmillan and Co., 1897; Royal Geographical Society, London; Cooper-Bridgeman Library. *Text:* Courtesy of the Geographical Magazine.

Sir Tatton Sykes: Sir Richard Sykes.

Thomas de Quincey: The Mansell Collection; Radio Times Hulton Picture Library; Popperfoto.

Ouida: Chatto and Windus; Punch; Radio Times Hulton Picture Library.

Squire Waterton: The Illustrated London News; 'Charles Waterton: his Home, Habits and Handiwork' by Richard Hobson, 1866; National Portrait Gallery, London.

Jack Mytton: The Mansell Collection.

William Beckford of Fonthill Abbey: Bath Municipal Libraries; 'The Gentleman's Magazine'; 'Delineations of Fonthill and its Abbey' by John Rutter, 1833; The Hamilton and Kinneil Estates.

Julia Margaret Cameron: Christie's, London; Victoria and Albert Museum, London; Radio Times Hulton Picture Library.

Algernon Charles Swinburne: Radio Times Hulton Picture Library; 'Swinburne' by Joan Overton Fuller, Chatto and Windus, 1968; 'Life of Swinburne' by Edmund Gosse, Macmillan and Co. Ltd., 1917; 'At The Pines' by Molly Panter-Downes, Hamish Hamilton Ltd., 1971.

Romeo Coates: 'European Magazine'; Victoria and Albert Museum, London; Endhoven Collection; The Mansell Collection.

Foreword

'England is the paradise of individuality, eccentricity, heresy, anomalies, hobbies and humours'; so wrote George Santayana in his essay on the British character. The theory that eccentricity is a peculiarly English trait is supported by Edith Sitwell in her book *English Eccentrics*, where she declares that 'Eccentricity exists particularly in the English and partly, I think, because of that peculiar and satisfactory knowledge of infallibility that is the hallmark and birthright of the British nation'.

Whatever the reasons, eccentricity has often proved to be a British trait and has certainly been aspired to by many members of that race who have regarded the norm as a dreary condition of life, better suited to the previous generation than to their own. But the true eccentric is, of course, a character who bears no relation to this. He is unconsciously out of tune with his age: he is what his contemporaries would regard as 'off-centre', whether in behaviour, attitudes or physical appearance.

In this illustrated collection of essays, we have assembled a wide variety of characters from different ages and backgrounds. Not all of them display 'eccentricities of genius', as Sam Weller chose to describe the quality to Mr Pickwick, but in the context of social history all are exceptional examples of their time, all are interesting and some, indeed, of great consequence. They include Mad Jack Mytton, the squire who drank eight bottles of port a day and set fire to his nightshirt to cure a fit of hiccups, and the ingenious Princess Caraboo, the servant-girl from Devon, an early confidence-trickster who stole the heart of Napoleon exiled on St Helena.

In an attempt to personalize the essays, the authors have almost without exception made their own choice of character with one proviso: that the reader should receive both amusement and instruction from their eccentricity. If at times the latter part of this provision has been fulfilled somewhat eccentrically, then that may be as it should be.

Lord Berners

During the summer months of 1935, a fantastic tower started to take shape on the crest of a wooded hillock above the market town of Faringdon. It rose to a height of some one hundred and forty feet and was topped by a great octagonal lantern, from which, after scrambling up a narrow spiral stair, one could gaze out for miles across the fields of several counties and, to the south, the Berkshire Downs and the White Horse of Uffington.

For several years the plans for its erection had been attended by a frenzy of protest and conflict, and the decision of the local council to withhold planning consent had been over-ridden by higher powers from the Ministry of Health. Amongst wild rumours, the furious complaints of the local gentry, and watched by the delighted eye of the Press, the tower grew higher; and by the end of the year the last great folly of the twentieth century was completed. The architect was Lord Gerald Wellesley, later Duke of Wellington, and the man to dream up, organize and finance the whole project was Gerald Tyrwhitt-Wilson, 14th Baron Berners. The folly was christened with a splendid party, and a neat notice adorned its entrance – 'MEMBERS OF THE PUBLIC COMMITTING SUICIDE FROM THIS TOWER DO SO AT THEIR OWN RISK'.

From his Palladian villa on the edge of Faringdon, where doves dyed to every shade of the rainbow fluttered over sloping lawns, and birds of paradise and whippets with diamond collars wandered amongst a priceless collection of treasures, Lord Berners remained unmoved by the storm. 'The great point of the tower', he stated firmly, 'is that it will be entirely useless', no doubt realizing that the very people who were now protesting so noisily would soon look upon their local landmark with pride. Flippancy, an art at which he excelled, was one of the methods whereby Lord Berners evaded the attention of bores. It was also, as is so often the case, a screen behind which his highly sensitive creative spirit could take refuge. He was a small, dapper man with a clipped moustache and a diffident manner, his bald head frequently covered by a black Homburg hat, and his appearance gave little clue to his identity. Artist, author and musician of sparkling talent, discerning collector, wit, and a brilliant social figure, he could have belonged to an altogether more romantic and patrician age.

Lord Berners (1883–1950). *Artist, author and musician of sparkling talent, discerning collector, wit and a brilliant social figure, he could have belonged to an altogether more romantic and patrician age.*

He was born in 1883 at Apley Park in Shropshire, the only child in a large and comfortable Victorian household. His world was peopled by a scatter-brained, hard-hunting mother, a worldly and intolerant father, bachelor uncles, an invalid aunt with a passion for Paris hats, and a crazed grandfather who spent all day groaning and cursing most horribly. More awe inspiring was his paternal grandmother, a truly terrible woman, in appearance 'not unlike Holbein's portrait of Bloody Mary with just a touch of Charley's Aunt', who spread about her a black cloud of gloom, bigotry and cheap Bibles. Her family commented that, although she might be a baroness in her own right, she was everything else in her own wrong. Intellectual and artistic pursuits were discouraged, and the only matters of importance, apart from those connected with the horse, were the narrow interests of the country. From where, one wonders, can all the wit and fantasy have come: perhaps the strain of gypsy blood, darkly rumoured to run in the family, was in some way responsible.

After a period at a private school of typical grimness, where the headmaster failed to notice any of the latent talents of his young pupil and merely observed that he needed 'bracing up', he moved on to Eton.

In *First Childhood*, he writes of his earlier years with a delicately barbed humour that is quite irresistible; *A Distant Prospect*, although still very funny in places, is a surprisingly moving account of how Eton inspired him with its beauty, and showed him a first glimpse of the fascinating worlds of scholarship, art and social grace. However, his career was, on the surface, unsuccessful. He did not shine at exams, hated organized games, and his non-conformity made him on the whole unpopular with the other boys who referred to him as 'The Newt'.

After some years on the Continent, studying languages in France, Italy and Germany, music at Dresden and Vienna, and art, he became Honorary Attaché to the Diplomatic Service in Constantinople and later, until 1920, in Rome. Here, although he started to emerge on one level as a cultured and cosmopolitan figure, he relieved the tedium of his work by composing delightfully silly limericks, in the vein:

> A thing that Uncle George detests
> Is finding mouse shit in his vests
> But what he even more abhors
> Is seeing Auntie in her drawers.

and indulging in a large number of practical jokes in which he took a positively artistic delight. One of the senior members of Chancery had a habit of stressing his remarks by snatching up his spectacles and placing them pompously upon the end of his nose. Maddened by this, Tyrwhitt (as he still was) prepared an

Lord Berners' set and costumes for 'Wedding Bouquet', *one of the great ballet successes of the period.*

elaborate booby trap, attaching the spectacles with hidden threads to all the desk paraphernalia so that with the next ponderous statement ink, blotter and papers cascaded to the floor.

Frederick Ashton, Lord Berners and Constant Lambert. *A man of exceptional artistic talents, it was perhaps in the field of music that Lord Berners aspired to the highest. His originality was widely acknowledged; he was, for example, the only English composer to be directly commissioned by Diaghilev.*

He never could resist deflating the pretentious or hypocritical. 'They can't have known who we were', exclaimed a tiresome woman acquaintance, on finding insufficient attention paid to her in a restaurant. 'And who were you?' enquired Lord Berners. 'He's always backing into the limelight', he complained of T. E. Lawrence, and of Salvador Dali:

> On the pale yellow sands
> There's a pair of Clasped Hands
> And an Eyeball entangled with String
>
> And a Bicycle Seat
> And a plate of Raw Meat
> And a Thing that is hardly a Thing.

In 1918 he inherited his title – he held later that this was only because three of his uncles fell off a bridge at the same time. In fact, he came into two titles (one of which dates back to the fifteenth century), three houses and a large fortune.

Lord Berners is sometimes referred to as a dilettante; perhaps his talents were so widespread that this was inevitable, and maybe too his wit and sense of fun tended to divert people (as he probably intended) from the more serious side of his nature.

However, in nothing that he attempted was he a mere amateur. His landscape paintings were highly accomplished and were well received by both public and critics; indeed, his first exhibition in London during the early thirties was sold out within the day. (His artistic talents were sometimes employed in a very different way. At Faringdon, in old volumes of the *Illustrated London News*, royal personages and society beauties sported moustaches, warts and double chins, whilst the most surprising statements issued from their lips.)

Besides the two volumes of autobiography mentioned earlier, he published six novels, mostly works of satire and fantasy. A shrewd perception and an eye for the absurd runs through them all; one cannot help laughing aloud as one reads of the rigid economies of rich Mrs Pontefract, and of the camel that formed an inconvenient attachment for the Vicar's wife. 'The canine characters in this story are entirely imaginary, and no reference is intended to any living dog', warns Lord Berners, and 'The author will be obliged if his friends will not attempt to recognize each other in these pages', although one doubts that his advice was followed.

But it was in the field of music that he aspired to the highest. At various times he studied under Casella, Stravinsky and Vaughan Williams. He was the only English composer to be directly commissioned by Diaghilev, and was a friend of Constant Lambert and William Walton. He worked incessantly, and his music is full of sparkle and gaiety and an impressive technical skill besides. Parody and irony are seldom absent: a romantic German song is interrupted on the piano by the imitation of a grunting pig, and a note of happy expectation creeps into *Funeral March for a Rich Aunt*.

As well as piano and orchestral work, and several songs, Lord Berners wrote an opera (performed in Paris in 1922) and five ballets. His *chef d'œuvre*, *The Triumph of Neptune*, was performed by the Diaghilev Company in 1926, with a scenario by Sacheverell Sitwell. Frederick Ashton, Cecil Beaton and Gertrude Stein worked with him in later compositions, and amongst the performers were Ninette de Valois, Helpmann and Fonteyn. In *Wedding Bouquet* he himself designed the costumes and sets.

· TONY · WYSARD'S · WAXWORKS ·

EXHIBIT
6

EMERALD LADY CUNARD · Mr SIDNEY BEER · LORD BERNERS

MUSIC PATRONS

Lady Cunard, great supporter of opera and herself a musician, Mr. Sidney Beer, whose name is so well known in the world of music, and Lord Berners, to complete this constellation, who is probably one of the most versatile geniuses in the world of art. He is the composer of many operas and ballets, an artist of no mean pretensions and an author of several very good books. Lord Berners is likewise a most hospitable host, as all who have ever been to Faringdon House, his Berkshire seat, have every good reason to know

Cartoon *from 'The Tatler', 22 June, 1938*

FARINGDON FOLLY   LORD BERNERS

YOU CAN BE SURE OF SHELL

Poster *painted by Lord Berners in 1936 as an advertisement for Shell, of Faringdon Folly, a tower about one hundred and forty feet in height which had been built the previous year despite much public protest. It was christened with a party and a neat notice adorned its entrance, 'Members of the public committing suicide from this tower do so at their own risk'. Lord Berners flippantly insisted that its great point was 'that it will be entirely useless'.*

Seldom can the audiences at Covent Garden and Sadlers Wells have laughed as delightedly as they did during these light-hearted and accomplished pieces, in which the Smart Set parade the Trouville beach attired in Edwardian bathing-dress, Oriental potentates descend from the sky in magnificent striped balloons, and Italian tenors mime impossibly romantic arias.

In his entry in *Who's Who*, Lord Berners listed his recreations as 'none', and this was not only flippancy. When not writing, painting or composing, he was cultivating another talent – the gift for friendship. Artistic and aristocratic circles mingled in his houses at Faringdon, London and on the Forum in Rome. The company was diverse, the conversation stimulating, and there was no room for the trivial or the tedious. In his company, people tended to feel on their best form.

16

The South Front of Faringdon House, *the seat of Lord Berners. His magnificent Palladian villa was enhanced by doves whose plumage was dyed to every shade of the rainbow.*

Bernard Shaw, Aldous Huxley, H. G. Wells and the Sitwells, were all frequent visitors; and Lady Sybil Colefax, and the strange Marchesa Casati with her orange-dyed hair, purple monkey and pet boa-constrictor, and Schiaparelli (who was borne off to a local Church Bazaar, and to everyone's delight encouraged to make several purchases at the second-hand clothes stall). 'There was hardly a moment when we were not lords and ladies . . .' wrote Gertrude Stein to Alice B. Toklas, '. . . there were so many orchids!' 'Rolls-Roycey', said D. H. Lawrence, less at ease.

The cuisine too was memorable, and Lord Berners was himself an inspired artist in the kitchen, in spite of a preference for poached eggs and vodka. He collected cooks, with whom he used to converse at length – 'A bored cook soon becomes a bad cook'.

Hunting neighbours might sometimes catch a glimpse of this intriguing world when they were invited to attend a play in the lakeside pavilion, or a Bank Holiday

Lord Berners

composer of the recently produced "Cupid and Psyche" shows ILLUSTRATED cameraman round his country home, explains below why there is a modern boom in ballet

THERE can be no doubt that ballet is now more appreciated in England than in any other country: that England is now the spiritual home of ballet.

Formerly the cult of a restricted public, it is acquiring every day a wider and more varied following of enthusiasts. Literature treating of the ballet grows apace.

Nearly every month brings a new book on the subject (often by people whose enthusiasm is their only merit) and soon libraries will be as cluttered with books on ballet as they formerly were with books on theology.

The modern type of ballet which, to borrow pictorial terminology, might be described as "genre" ballet, was invented by Diaghileff. Originally a rebel offshoot of the Imperial Russian Ballet, it broke away from the classical tradition

and then assumed new and more exciting forms.

It progressed and developed, while retaining many ballets of classical type, from *Carneval* and *Spectre de la Rose* to ballets such as *Sacre du Printemps* and *Pas d'Acier*.

Serious composers of every country, Stravinsky, Ravel, Richard Strauss, de Falla, wrote music for it. Painters such as Picasso, Derain, Utrillo, designed costumes and scenery. This was all through the initiative of Diaghileff, and his death seemed at first as though it would be the death blow to ballet.

But, after a chaotic interval, a new order became established. Sadler's Wells is now the principal home of ballet in England.

It is an institution of which every English lover of ballet has reason to be proud. For no other ballet company in the world could boast of so gifted a trio as Ninette de Valois, Frederick

Ashton and Constant Lambert, in charge of the choreography and the music, combined with a band of dancers displaying such individual technique, such fascinating and varied personalities.

One of the reasons for the great popularity of ballet at the present moment is perhaps that it is one of the most palpable manifestations of " Art for Art's Sake."

It represents what left-wing highbrows call "escapist art" in its purest form. There is in ballet no insidious motive of edification and uplift. And although ballet companies may call themselves "educational" their primary object is, or should be, to entertain rather than educate.

It is to ballet that you may flee from the wrath to come and from the wrath that seems almost at hand. In these troublous times we may at least escape for an hour or two to Sadler's Wells and other places where there is ballet.

(Continued overleaf)

May 20, 1939—ILLUSTRATED

Page from 'Illustrated', *20 May, 1939, from an article in which Lord Berners explains the modern boom in ballet. Lord Berners possessed another car to the one photographed here, an old-fashioned Rolls Royce fitted at the back with a spinet.*

fair, complete with circus, merry-go-round, steam organ and brass band; or perhaps a firework party, where guests were encouraged to bring effigies of their worst enemies to burn – not more than six each.

Sometimes, too, his old-fashioned Rolls Royce, fitted at the back with a spinet, might flash past them along the Berkshire lanes, and a horrible idiot-mask designed by Oliver Messel would peer through the windows. He must have seemed to them a strangely incomprehensible figure, a little formidable, although always scrupulously polite, the Homburg hat giving place as he grew older to a black skull cap, or, on occasions, a scarlet woollen pixie hood.

He held no political creed, nor did he follow any religious denomination. Edith Sitwell tells of an occasion when, during a luncheon party, Lord Berners' butler came into the dining-room and said, 'The gentleman outside asks if you would be good enough to sign this, m'lord'. The document in question read: 'AN APPEAL TO GOD THAT WE MIGHT HAVE PEACE IN OUR TIME'. 'It's no good', said Berners sadly, 'he won't know who I am – probably has never heard of me'.

Of course, a quantity of anecdotes gathered round his reputation. In his book *The Four Continents*, Sir Osbert Sitwell relates how they were staying at the same time in a hotel in Greece, where the proprietor was locally rumoured to be a werewolf. Hearing him approach his room in the early hours of the morning, Lord Berners threw open his door and fell upon all fours in his pyjamas, barking wildly. However, the sinister man walked calmly past, with a 'Good morning, m'lord'.

Lord Berners and Gertrude Stein studying a score. '*There was hardly a moment when we were not lords and ladies . . .*' wrote Gertrude Stein to Alice B. Toklas, describing her experiences as one of Lord Berners' guests, '. . . *there were so many orchids*'.

He was also rumoured to make a collection of other people's visiting-cards, which he would hoard until a suitable occasion arose for their use. Having with characteristic generosity lent his villa in Rome to friends on honeymoon, he forwarded to his butler there a selection of cards carefully chosen to include only Society's most celebrated bores, and instructed him to place a few of these each day on the tray in the hall. One wonders how long the couple spent in a fever of apprehension about the callers that never materialized, before they realized who was behind it all.

Through the twenties and thirties, the Press regaled the public with many highly coloured reports of his pastimes: he had set up a ranch in Spain for breeding fighting bulls, he was training a pack of hounds to forage for truffles in the Berkshire woods, he was to attend a fancy dress ball disguised as a monkey-bride. They also did their best to marry him off, and once even got as far as front page headlines about a forthcoming engagement to Miss Violet Trefusis. But the news was only an elaborate joke. It had got rather out of hand when a reporter, telephoning him for information, was mistaken for a jesting friend, and was given a long and well-spiced interview.

Lord Berners remained a bachelor all his life. But he was quite happy to fill in a questionnaire on the six requirements for a happy marriage:

> A short memory
> A long purse
> Infinite credulity
> No sense of humour
> A combative nature
> The man should be a man, and the
> Woman a woman, or vice versa.

In spite of all the fun and gaiety he remained, as his close friends well knew, an essentially private person, self-critical and introspective, who laughed so as to keep melancholy at bay. But although he might need the presence of friends, he was selective in the company he kept, and Constant Lambert describes his method of keeping a railway carriage to himself: 'Donning black spectacles, he would, with a look of fiendish expectation, beckon in the passers by. Those isolated figures who took the risk became so perturbed by his habit of reading the papers upside down and taking his temperature every five minutes that they invariably got out at the next station'.

The Second World War with its horrors and implications of irrevocable change, upset him deeply, and as the forties drew on, his output of work grew smaller and finally stopped. He withdrew further into melancholy and ill-health.

Tea at Faringdon House. *From left to right: Bubbles Radclyffe; Penelope Chetwode's horse; Penelope Chetwode; Robert Heber-Percy; Lord Berners.*

'All inspirational sources seem to have dried up', he wrote to a friend. But his sense of humour was not quite extinguished. One weekend when he was more than usually silent and morose, the large house-party asked each other where it would all end. Then in the middle of the night there was a deafening explosion downstairs, as though of a shot gun. Horrified, everyone rushed out of their bedrooms in nocturnal disarray, to find that Lord Berners had popped a paper bag in the hall.

When he died in 1950, his friends mourned an unforgettable person and the fantasy world he had created. The wider public, more fickle, has tended to lose sight of the creative artist behind the reputation of the wit and humorist. But no doubt with posterity a most unusual and vivid life will be seen in a clearer perspective. As he said in his own epitaph:

> Here lies Lord Berners,
> One of the learners.
> His great love of learning
> May earn him a burning.
> But praise to the Lord
> He never was bored!

Capaboo

Oh where did she come from? and who can she be? Did she fall from the sky? did she rise from the sea?   WILLIAM HONE EVERYDAY BOOK 1864

On an April evening in 1817 an event occurred which set the whole of England talking: the arrival, in Almondsbury in Gloucestershire, of a strange young woman dressed in an Asiatic fashion and speaking no English. She was five foot two, with black hair and eyes, full lips and a rounded chin, and she wore a black shawl twisted turban-like around her head, a black and red shawl draped over her shoulders, and a black dress with a muslin frill around the neck. On her feet were stout leather shoes, and on her legs black worsted stockings. Her hands were clean and white and did not look as if she had ever had to work.

Travel-stained and weary, the girl entered a cottage in the village and made signs that she wanted food and a bed for the night. She pointed to a couch in the corner of the room, but the cottager, alarmed by her gestures and the fact that she did not seem to understand what he was saying, sent immediately for the Overseer of the Poor. When the Overseer of the Poor arrived, he offered her sixpence, but she rejected it, so he 'referred to Mr Worrall, a Magistrate of the County', for his advice.

Mr Worrall was curious, and asked for the strange young woman to be brought to him, but for some reason the girl was reluctant to go and had to be forcibly persuaded, and when they reached Knole Park, where Mr and Mrs Worrall awaited her, she hung back and refused to enter the door for some time.

Mrs Worrall was fascinated by the girl. Neither she nor Mr Worrall could understand what she was saying, and she looked blankly at them when they spoke to her; but by signs they made her turn out her pockets, which contained a few halfpence and a bad sixpence. Next they wanted to see what she carried in a small bundle she was holding, but when she opened it there was nothing of interest: a few necessities and a piece of soap pinned up in a bit of linen.

Mrs Worrall sent the romantic stranger for the night to the public house in the village, accompanied by her maid and footman, to see that she was provided with a good supper and a comfortable bed.

After she had eaten, the landlady took her to the room in which she was to

Mary Wilcox.
of Witheridge, Devonshire.
alias
CARABOO.
Drawn & Engraved by N. Branwhite.

Frontispiece from 'Caraboo: a Narrative of a Singular Imposition', *published in 1817 by Allman of London.*
The engraving shows Caraboo dressed in the clothes in which it is recorded that she arrived at Almondsbury.

sleep, but the girl appeared reluctant to use the bed and pointed to the floor, so the horrified landlady called her daughter to come in and show the foreigner what beds were for. 'Upon the landlady's little girl getting into the bed and making her understand the comfort of it, she undressed and after kneeling and appearing to say her prayers, she consented to lie on the bed'.

At seven the next morning Mrs Worrall arrived, carrying a change of linen for the girl. She was closely followed by the clergyman of the parish, who hurried in, clutching in his arms a great quantity of books, from which he hoped to discover some clue to the strange woman's identity. The girl, who had been looking sad, became animated on seeing the pictures in the books, and 'gave the spectators to understand that she had some knowledge of the prints which were descriptive of China; but made signs that it was not a boat, but a ship, which had brought her to this country'.

Mrs Worrall, enthralled by the mystery surrounding the romantic female, decided to take her back to Knole. On arrival at Knole the girl was taken straight to the housekeeper's room where the servants were at breakfast, and since it was Good Friday there were hot cross buns upon the table. The girl 'took one, and after looking at it earnestly, she cut off the cross, and placed it in her bosom'.

Mrs Worrall then set off for church, where she meditated on the situation, and on her return she summoned the girl to her and said, 'My good young woman, I very much fear that you are imposing upon me, and that you understand and can answer me in my own language; if so, and distress has driven you to this expedient, make a friend of me. I am a female as yourself, and can feel for you, and will give you money and clothes, and will put you on your journey, without disclosing your conduct to anyone; but it must be on condition that you speak the truth. If you deceive me, I think it right to inform you that Mr Worrall is a Magistrate, and has the power of sending you to prison, committing you to hard labour, and passing you as a vagrant to your own parish'.

The girl's face remained totally blank. She did not appear to have understood a word of what Mrs Worrall had been saying, and Mrs Worrall was convinced. Taking a pen in her hand she tried to find out the stranger's name by writing her own down on paper several times and showing it to the girl, crying out 'Worrall! Worrall!' as she did so. She then handed the girl the pen, but the girl shrank back and shook her head, saying 'Caraboo! Caraboo!' several times and pointing to herself.

At dinner Caraboo 'declined all animal food, and took nothing to drink but water, shewing much distaste at meat, beer, cyder, etc'. It was found later that she would only eat food prepared with her own hands, in the Hindu style.

On Saturday she was taken before the Magistrates at the Council House in Bristol to be examined; but they could find out nothing about her, and had her

Caraboo, Princess of Javasu, alias Mary Baker, an etching by E. Bird showing her in an imaginary tropical setting, adorned as she might have been in her own country. Coming anonymously as she did from a kingdom whose location wavered from China to the Indies, with a particular predilection for Sumatra, her arrival caused considerable surprise and was testified to by a number of fashionable artists.

committed to St Peter's Hospital, the Bristol workhouse. Here she refused to eat or drink or sleep in any of the beds, though the matron cooked eggs and other delicacies for her and 'the most humane attentions were shewn her'.

From all over England people came to visit Caraboo in the hope of being the first to discover who she was. They wrote to Mrs Worrall telling her their conclusions and offering their suggestions; one gentleman imagined he had made the discovery that when Caraboo cried 'Caraboo' and pointed to herself, she was not

26

telling Mrs Worrall her name, but merely her country of origin. She came, he thought, from Karabouh on the eastern coast of the Caspian Sea.

After three days Mrs Worrall took Caraboo away from St Peter's and installed her in Samuel Worrall's office in Bristol, under the care of her housekeeper. Here, all was revealed. A Portuguese, who gave his name as Manuel Eynesso, appeared, and after listening to Caraboo for a short time, he told the delighted Mrs Worrall that he could understand every word she spoke. She was a person of great consequence in her own country; she came from an island in the West Indies; she had been brought to England against her will and then deserted, and her language was a mixture of languages used on the coast of Sumatra. Having said this, Manuel Eynesso disappeared and was never heard of again.

Mrs Worrall promptly took Caraboo back to Knole with her, and in the weeks that followed learned gentlemen visited Knole and compiled a list of Caraboo's words and their meanings – for they were always consistent; they puzzled over her writing, and they wrote down her story for the world to read.

RACTERS made use of by CARABOO, and her AUTOGRAPH of MARY BAKE
☞ The lettered reader will perceive a few perfectly-formed and conjoined Arabic charactes
need not to be added, that she copied them from those which some Oriental Scholar wn
efore her.

Mary Baker Devonshire

NUMERICAL CHARACTERS, with their Significations, made use of by CARABOO.

1		Eze
2		Duce
3		Trua
4		Tan
5		Zennee
6		Seudee
7		Tam
8		Nunta
9		Berteeu
10		Tashman
11		Limmenee
12		Judgbennee
13		Artinne
14		Ferney
15		Fissmen
		Infuse red paint.

LEFT: *Characters used by Caraboo which led to widespread dispute as to her country of origin. A certain Dr Wilkinson of Bath wrote to the 'Bath Chronicle': 'All the assistance to be derived from a Polyglot Bible, Fry's "Pantographia", or Dr. Hager's "Elementary Characters of the Chinese", did not enable us to ascertain either the nature of her language, or the country to which she belongs'.*

RIGHT: *Numerical characters used by Caraboo. From the various accounts of Caraboo, we gather that she carried about her a cord, knotted at one end like a Chinese abacus, followed by the sliding beads. China was one of the countries from which she was thought to have originated.*

A VOCABULARY OF WORDS, WITH THEIR MEANINGS, MADE USE OF BY CARABOO.

Allah Tallah	God	Oree	Onions
Samen	Heaven	Savoo	a Knife
Tarsa	Earth	Foso	a Fork
Mordains	the Malay	Oser	Salt
Buis, or Bugos	any Wild People	Makey	Pepper
Manjintoo	Gentlemen	Arra	an Eclipse
Lazor	Ladies	Sanatoo	the Sun
Makrittoo	Servant Men	Toree	a Stone
Somens	Servant Women	Bardoo	Dead
Justo or Justu	Doctor	Smache	Cayenne
Kala	Time	Botee	an Arrow
Alkader	Lot, Destiny	Doteau	Gold Dust
Mono	Morning	Sirrea	Mother of Pearl
Anna	Night	Nontee	an Orange
Vellee	Bed	Botin	the Head
Apa	Fire	Nater	the Arm
Ana	Water	Nease	the Foot
Savee	Rain	Tenzenee	a Sail
Meller	Yes	Tuzar	a Ship
Beek	Good	Bosve	a Boat
No bo	No good	Toose	to swim
Dosi	Dinner	Paza	Peacock's Feathers
Sacco	Supper		
Ake Brasidoo	Come to Breakfast		a Word in common
Ake Dosi	Come to Dinner		use in Malay, li-
Ake Sacco	Come to Supper	Puloponnaung	terally the Betel
Zee	Tea		Nut Island in the
Suso	Sugar		Straits of Malac-
Passa	Flour		ca
Mo	Milk	Khalifaton	Words to which she
Bras	Rice	Kader	affixed no deter-
Pakey	Child	Zimam	minate meaning.
Vatan	Gown	Ziban	
Mozum	Fish	Prabha	Head
Tamah	Fowl	Indue	her Father's Coun-
Rampue or Rambu	a Pidgeon		try
Nee	Egg	Induis	her Mother's Coun-
Archee	Potatoe		try
		Iuju Jagoos	Do not be afraid.

THE FOLLOWING WERE THE FEW GYPSEY WORDS, WHICH SHE USED.

Mosha	a Man	Tanner	a Sixpence
Raglish	a Woman	Bob	a Shilling
Gosha	a Landlady	Junk	two Shillings
Tanee	a Halfpenny	Bub	five Shillings.
Win	a Penny		

A Vocabulary of words, with their meanings, made use of by Caraboo *indicating some of the problems met by the linguists who were determined to attribute a country and nationality to Caraboo. She wrote from left to right and asserted that in her country, a camel's hair pencil and a species of papyrus were used rather than pen and paper.*

She was the daughter of a person of rank, and a Princess. She was of Chinese origin, though her mother was Malay. She came from an island named Javasu, and had been captured by pirates while walking in her garden. On the voyage they had exchanged her with the Captain of a Brig for a sack of gold dust. Having suffered ill treatment on this vessel she jumped overboard one night and swam to the nearest shore, which happened to be that of England. When she jumped into the sea she had been wearing a gown and a shawl of rich material worked in

28

gold, but these she had exchanged at the house of an Englishwoman, whose door was painted green. This woman had given her the clothes she was wearing when she walked into the village of Almondsbury.

Her story was most interesting, and Mrs Worrall bought her some calico 'for her to make a dress in the style she was accustomed to wear'. This turned out to be 'very short in the petticoat, with sleeves uncommonly wide and long enough to reach the ground, but only half-scored up and confined at the wrists'. With this dress she wore open sandals and no stockings.

At Knole she made herself at home and kept the servants and Mrs Worrall in a perpetual state of tension. On days when she felt like going to war, she would arm herself with a gong on her back, a tambourine in her hand, a sword by her side (a stick served the purpose) and a bow and arrow slung over her shoulder, while her hair was skewered on top of her head and dressed with bows and feathers. Beating the gong, sounding the tambourine, leaping and prancing and firing off arrows, she was the wonder of the neighbourhood. The tenants and their daughters grew very fond of her, and she would often visit them for tea.

She could dance with great dexterity, holding up one foot and whirling in a sort of waltz. She fenced with Mr Worrall, and he found it difficult to disarm her; she swam like a fish and climbed trees like a monkey.

Once, when Mrs Worrall was at a wake in the parish, she disappeared completely. The gardens and park were searched, but no trace of her was found. When they had despaired of ever seeing her again, she was discovered sitting comfortably in the top of a tree. She explained that she had climbed the tree 'in order to escape contamination from men' since there were no females in the house at the time.

A certain Dr Wilkinson, a noted scientist, wrote several letters to the *Bath Chronicle* in the hope that someone might recognize the description of Caraboo, and in one of them he laments that 'all the assistance to be derived from the Polyglot Bible, Fry's Pantographia, or Dr Hager's Elementary Characters of the Chinese, does not enable us to ascertain either the nature of her language, or the country to which she belongs . . . her letter has been shown to every person in Bristol and Bath versed in Oriental literature, but without success. A copy was sent to India House, and submitted by the Chairman of the Company to Mr Raffles, one of the best Oriental scholars, yet he could not decipher it. The original letter was sent to Oxford, and the members of that University denied it being the character of any language . . .'

In June, Caraboo vanished from Knole and was discovered by the same Dr Wilkinson in Bath. He took her to the Pack Horse Inn to rest, while he

View of Knole Park, Almondsbury, *taken from the north, home of Mr Worrall, a magistrate in Gloucestershire, and his wife who first befriended Caraboo and gave her shelter at Knole.*

alerted Mrs Worrall as to her whereabouts, and here she was found by a host of fashionable ladies who had heard rumours that the enchanting Caraboo was in town. They flocked to the inn, and one of their number carried her off to her house and installed her in the drawing-room.

When Mrs Worrall arrived, what a sight met her eyes. 'The drawing-room was crowded with fashionable visitants', says a letter, 'all eager to be introduced to the fascinating Princess. There was one fair female kneeling before her, another taking her by the hand, another begging for a kiss! And then it was – Poor Dear Creature! What shall we do to make her comfortable! Poor Dear Creature!'

Having found Caraboo, Mrs Worrall took her back to Knole, while Dr Wilkinson set off to London to beg the directors of India House to try to discover more about her; but as Dr Wilkinson set off for London, a certain Mrs Neale set off for Almondsbury.

She had read Dr Wilkinson's letters to the *Bath Chronicle*, and had recognized a picture of Caraboo to be none other than that of an erstwhile lodger of hers who had wished to make five pounds to pay her passage to Philadelphia on an emigrant ship, and had decided to do so by begging in the guise of a foreigner.

From Mrs Neale, Mrs Worrall learnt that Caraboo's real name was Mary Baker and that she was the daughter of a cobbler in Witheredge, in Devonshire. She had worked as a servant-girl since the age of sixteen and had travelled widely, changing situations with great frequency; leaving one because the fire smoked, and another because they would not raise her wages from eight pence to one shilling a week. She had dressed as a man and been asked to join a band of foot-pads, had had a baby which had died, and been for six months at the Magdalen Home for Reformed Prostitutes under the impression that it was a nunnery.

Mrs Worrall forgave her, for she had become very fond of Mary. She paid for the girl to sail to Philadelphia on the *Robert and Ann*, which carried a mixed cargo of pig-iron, mallets, glass bottles, salt, cheese, tripe, a bedstead, two fowling pieces, and, of course, Mary.

In the course of the voyage it was reported in *The Bristol Journal* of September 1817 that Caraboo had leapt into a rowing boat, the ship having been driven off course, and rowed to St Helena. There she met Napoleon, who had 'embraced her with every demonstration of enthusiastic rapture' and asked Sir Hudson Lowe, the Governor, if he could not get the Pope to dissolve his marriage to Maria Louisa and let him marry the enchanting Caraboo instead.

Seven years later, Mary returned to England and exhibited herself in New Bond Street, Bath; admittance charge, one shilling, to see the famous Princess Caraboo of Javasu. Here, dressed in strange clothes, and with feathers in her hair, she waited. But few people came. Mary had been a nine-days wonder, nothing more; and she ended her days importing and selling leeches to the Infirmary Hospital and drugstores in Bristol.

Aleister Crowley

Alesteir Crowley, the mystic and poet who died in 1947, is reputed to have admitted on his deathbed, 'I am perplexed'. This must surely be the reaction of anyone, either his contemporary or successor, who has attempted to make a study of his life. How far the confusion has been caused by unprecedented interest resulting in conflicting reports on the part of the Press and between his friends, or by the man himself, will always be a subject for conjecture.

Crowley's beginning was doubtless as perplexing to him as his end. His official biographer, John Symonds, tells us that his earliest recorded life transpired among a 'Council of Masters', shortly before the time of Mohammed. His duty as one of its members was to convert the Western world to Oriental beliefs at the same time as restoring paganism in its purest form. At a later stage he believed that he was reincarnated as the pleasure-loving Alexander VI, who was elected to the papacy through bribery but who, according to Crowley, failed to succeed in 'crowning the Renaissance through not being wholly purified in [my] personal character'.

Crowley describes his ancestry in his autobiography, *The Spirit of Solitude: An Autohagiography*, in more actual, if no less romantic, terms. He wished it to be thought that his family was connected with that of Louise Renée de Kéroualle but, if there is any truth in this assertion, the connection must have been exceedingly tenuous, his own father being a Kentish brewer and a fervent follower of the Plymouth brethren.

Crowley was educated at two schools, Tonbridge and Malvern; at the latter he attempted to verify the legend of a cat's nine lives by scientific experiment.

> I caught a cat and having administered a large dose of arsenic, I chloroformed it, hanged it above the gas jet, stabbed it, cut its throat, smashed its skull, and when it had been pretty thoroughly burnt, drowned it and threw it out of the window that the fall might remove the ninth life. The operation was successful. I was genuinely sorry for the animal; I simply forced myself to carry out the experiment in the interests of pure science.

He went up to Trinity College, Cambridge, in 1896 leaving Cambridge at the end of the nineties. He came to London with a fortune of £40,000 with which to indulge his predilection for frivolity and the pursuit of the occult. One of his first assaults against the establishment was to lampoon Queen Victoria. In language which many would have considered offensive, he described her as a fat German *hausfrau* and pronouncing all Hanoverians to be usurpers, he joined the Carlist conspirators, was knighted by Don Carlos and declared that – under the Salic Law – all Victorian knighthoods were invalid.

His poetry – which he had printed privately – also offended public sensibility as did the sensational poetry of Swinburne, Baudelaire and *The Yellow Book* of much the same time. *The Sword of Song* is described by some as the outstanding book of his early period. Its outward appearance was startling. It was large quarto in size, printed in red and black throughout and bound in navy blue with a gold design on the front consisting of the number '666', another of his pseudonyms, repeated three times in the form of a square. Sixty-two pages consisted of poetry, and the remaining one hundred and thirty-two of notes on the poems, and appendices which were mainly an exposition and criticism of Buddhist philosophy.

The Mark of the Beast *within the seven-pointed star of Babylon. The sun in the arms of the moon symbolizes Babylon and the Beast conjoined. The sun is the creative force in the universe (macrocosm) and the Phallus in man (microcosm). Crowley liked to identify himself with the Beast whose number is the number of a man, six hundred and three score six. It was perhaps the mystery of this number which determined his strange choice.*

Another book from Crowley's early period is a faithful day-by-day account in a series of sonnets of the enactment of an adultery in Honolulu. It was entitled *Alice, an Adultery* and published by the Society for the Propogation of Religious Truth at Boleskine, Inverness, which caused the *Glasgow Herald* to remark: 'We confess to being so dense as to miss the essentially religious purpose of the book . . . But the power of many of the sonnets is undeniable . . .'

The number of aliases which Crowley assumed in the course of his life were legion: they included A. E. Crawley, the Comte de St Germain, Count von

Zonaref, Alastair McGregor and the Earl of Middlesex. It was as Count Svareff that he lived in a flat in Chancery Lane which he decorated as a magical temple and, after buying an estate at Boleskine in Inverness-shire, as the Laird of Boleskine that he frequently appeared in smarter public places.

His dress in those days tended to be a kilt or, on a recorded visit to the Café Royal, the full paraphernalia of a Scottish chieftain. At the Café Royal again he caused a stir of equal magnitude when he appeared in evening-dress wearing a metal butterfly as a codpiece. The latter had originally been used by Crowley to placate the police in Paris who had refused to allow Epstein's nude statue of Oscar Wilde to be unveiled to the public. By a stratagem 'in the interests of art', he had affixed the metal butterfly to the offending parts in much the same way that fig leaves had been affixed to early statues in Wilde's own lifetime by his countrymen. A further distinction to his appearance must have been lent by his teeth, which were filed into points *à la vampire*.

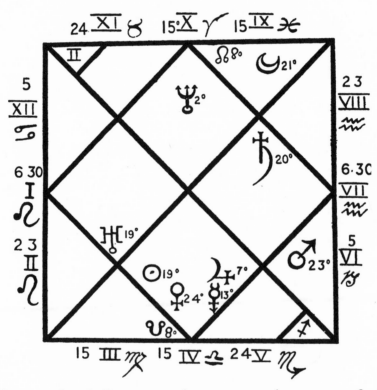

Crowley's horoscope. *Born, by his own account, between 11 p.m. and 12 p.m. on 12 October, 1875, at Leamington Spa, his horoscope was described by astrologer Rupert Gleadow as having 'nothing particularly devilish about it. . . . It is not so obviously bad as the horoscope of Luther which the Pope's astrologer published in the hope of proving that Luther would go to Hell'.*

Soon after Crowley came down from Cambridge many of the legends with which he is now associated rapidly increased in circulation. He climbed the soft chalk of Beachy Head to the complete astonishment of the natives no less than of experienced climbers. He began achieving climbing records in Cumberland, in Wales and in the Alps to the surprise and discomfort of that respectable bastion, the Alpine Club, whose members' prowess to date had never been seriously challenged. From time to time he mysteriously disappeared, to reappear in his old haunts looking considerably younger and even more sardonic, witty, vituperative and 'evil'. On such occasions he would walk across the Sahara, climb the Himalayas, where *John Bull* reports that, running short of provisions, he killed two of his native carriers and cut them up for food, lived as a Yogi in Ceylon, walked across China and explored Mexican volcanoes. The more envious followers of his career said that he practised physical vampirism or that he had discovered the Elixir of Life, either alternative to account for his physical vitality. The last of these two unfounded reports he attempted to substantiate and profit from in the 1930s by trying, and failing, to persuade a friend, Alan Burnett-Rae, to market 'The Elixir of Rejuvenation' under his auspices.

Rumour was also rife that Crowley knew how to turn base metals into gold; this would have accounted for his wealth, as evinced by his sumptuously produced, privately printed books, his love of good food and travel. Yet another faction insisted that he obtained money from wealthy women by blackmail, intimidation and worse.

Members of the public walked into his publisher's office uttering cryptic warnings. One helpful and interested party advised, 'Always cross your fingers when you speak to Alesteir Crowley'. His own fingers were crossed all the while he was there.

Crowley aroused such unprecedented interest and dispute within his own lifetime that a supporter, P. R. Stephenson, was incited to write a book in his defence which was published some seventeen years before Crowley died. This he entitled, *The Legend of Alesteir Crowley, being a Study of the Documentary Evidence Relating to a Campaign of Personal Vilification Unparalleled in Literary History*. The contemporary quotations which Stephenson selects and disputes range from 'England's worst man' (*John Bull*, 1929) to 'This man Crowley is one of the most sinister figures of modern times. He is a drug fiend, an author of vile books, the spreader of obscene practices. Yet such is his intellectual attainment and mental fascination that he is able to secure reputable publishers for his works and attract to him men and women of means and position' (*Sunday Express*, 1923).

To the indictments to which the *Sunday Express* subjected him, accusations were added by other members of the Press. He was described as pro-German, a drug trafficker and addict and the owner of 'an abode of love' with white slave implications. In each instance, Crowley provided just the necessary point of departure for these attacks.

He declared himself pro-German and pro-Irish in the First World War almost as an act of schoolboy perversity, reacting furiously against those super-patriots who blackguarded Wagner and Nietzsche for being German and stampeded the English nation into hysteria for military purposes. Spending most of the war in America, he travelled extensively, canoeing up the Hudson River, living as a hermit on Œsopus Island – always restless. In New York he enjoyed a number of light-hearted, practical jokes, one being his 'Declaration of Irish Independence' on 3 July, 1915, when he threw his British passport (an old envelope) into the river harbour proclaiming Irish independence from the foot of the Statue of Liberty to attendant publicity.

Another scheme to raise publicity was evolved by Crowley in an attempt to increase the story-line of a friend's book. They placed numerous small advertisements in provincial American papers announcing that the author would pay a reward of $10,000 to anyone who would recover for him the image, in its undamaged form, of Kwannon which they described as having been stolen from Sun Yat Sen at Shanghai on 13 June, 1904. The scheme was so successful that at least six hundred newspaper stories, many of them full-page and all of them full of the wildest inventions and speculation, appeared in the American Press. American reporters even called on the innocent President Sun Yat Sen in China to ask for his version and were dismayed when he discounted the tale as totally unfounded and ridiculous.

At the time of Prohibition, Crowley organized a substitute drinks party in New York called a 'Benzine Jag'. Invitations were issued in the following form:

JULY 1st. JOYFUL CELEBRATION. The Grand Master invites the representatives of the Press, the Prohibition Movement, the Pulpit, Poetry and the Police to join in the inaugural festival of the BENZINE JAG 9 p.m., July 1, No. 63 Washington Square. Love is the Law, Love under Will.

At much the same time Crowley became a painter and created a sensation in Greenwich Village by inserting the following advertisement in the daily press:

WANTED

DWARFS, HUNCHBACKS, Tattooed Women, Harrison Fisher Girls, Freaks of All Sorts, Coloured Women, only if exceptionally ugly or deformed, to pose for artist. Apply by letter with photograph. Box 707.

36

The Entrance to the Waste Land. *A finely executed pen and ink sketch by Crowley showing a characteristically debauched figure in the foreground guarding the entrance to a mythical Waste Land.*

When questioned by a reporter as to what sort of artist he was, he replied, 'Oh, I don't know just what to call myself. I'd say off-hand, that I was an old master . . .' A contemporary has actually vouched for his considerable ability, observing at the same time the macabre quality of his work. 'If he might have said "Evil, be thou my God", he might equally have pronounced that "Truth was Ugliness and Ugliness Truth" as far as art was concerned'.

Aleisteir Crowley. *Poet, mountaineer and drug addict, he was reviled by the press for his notorious black magic masses and his orgies. His two marriages ended unhappily and five of his mistresses committed suicide but to his followers, who still exist, he was a Messiah.*

According to Crowley's own works and supported by reported conversations, his friend, Alan Burnett-Rae, has declared that his great interests in life were a perverse sort of mysticism and sex. 'As to the first it seemed simply to consist of a cult of blasphemy in which he saw himself as a type of Anti-Christ . . . On one occasion my father . . . came to visit me and, on learning that Crowley lived in the house, expressed horror. It seems he had heard a story from one of his patients to the effect that Crowley and his disciples had broken into a church in Brussels by night and celebrated a "Mass" where the altar consisted of a naked woman on her hands and knees'.

During his five years in America, Crowley seemed to work out the ethical implications of his religion. When he returned to Europe in 1919 to live in a villa which he called 'The Abbey of Thelema', at Cefalu in Sicily, he had come to believe seriously that the War signified the breakdown of Christian civilization; that it was his duty to instruct people with a new ethical code whose basic theme was 'Do What Thou Wilt', a possible transcription from Rabelais' *Fay ce que vouldras*.

Since Alesteir Crowley welcomed both sexes to the Abbey to live in accordance with Thelemite principles, he soon laid himself open to the charge of establishing a 'love cult' or a 'free love' colony. The reputation of the colony was further shattered by the death of a young disciple, Raoul Loveday. Some witnesses testified that he had died of enteric fever following the drinking of unfiltered water, against which he had been specifically warned by Crowley; others that he had contracted a fatal disease after drinking the blood of a sacrificed cat. Whatever the truth, the first version seems the more likely. James Douglas of the *Sunday Express* made further journalistic currency out of Crowley with a full-length feature in the edition of 25 February, 1923. Among many other wild accusations, he claimed the following:

> Children under ten, whom the Beast keeps at the 'Abbey', are made to witness horrible sex debauches unbelievably revolting. Filthy incense is burned and cakes made of goats' blood and honey are consumed in the windowless room where the Beast conducts his rites. The rest of the time he lies in a room hung with obscene pictures collected from all over the world, saturating himself with drugs.

Crowley seriously believed that his establishment was designed for the purpose of bending the world to his demoniac vision . . . 'And my house', he declared, 'is going to be the Whore's Hell, a secret place of the quenchless fire of love and the eternal torment of love'. This vision was finally and abruptly ended on the night of 1 December, 1947, in a small room in Hastings where, of myocardial degeneration and chronic bronchitis, this extraordinary Englishman died, leaving beneath his pillow 'a parchment talisman consecrated for a great treasure'.

The Earl Bishop of Deppy

It was a much repeated eighteenth-century adage that the human race could be divided into three categories – 'men, women and Herveys' – and there was no member of this extraordinary family who did more to confirm people in this belief than Frederick Hervey, Earl of Bristol and Bishop of Derry.

He was born in 1730, was ordained at the age of twenty-four and became in turn Bishop of Cloyne, in Ireland, and then of Derry, before inheriting the earldom. He spent most of his life travelling round the Continent, and the huge number of hotels which took the name Bristol bear witness to his energy. He was intensely curious about everything and everybody he saw. He collected works of art with avidity and a certain lack of discrimination to adorn the great houses which were being built in Ireland and England in his absence. His collections were twice confiscated in time of war, but still he persevered. He himself was imprisoned and escaped packed in a hamper. Everywhere he was pointed at for his odd dress and outspoken remarks. He dabbled endlessly and fruitlessly in foreign politics, and eventually he died in a peasant's outhouse.

To his contemporaries, a man's eccentricity is the measure by which his character and actions deviate from the accepted standards of his own time. To us, it is also the measure by which they may deviate from the accepted standards of *our* own time, which may be very different. Thus a man may seem eccentric to his contemporaries and relatively normal to a later generation and vice versa.

The true eccentric, however, has a nature so singular that it is somehow at odds, though often for quite different reasons, with every generation. The Earl Bishop of Derry was one of these. A man of great talent and wide interests, he carried every enthusiasm to excess, and by this process of exaggeration distorted perfectly acceptable features of his personality into a caricature.

Thirty years after the Earl's death, Charles Lever wrote a novel called *The Bramleighs of Bishop's Folly* in which he described a character based on Bristol with some insight:

> He had great taste, which had been cultivated by foreign travel, and having an ample fortune, he was able to indulge in many whims and caprices, by which some were led to doubt of his sanity; but others who judged him better

Downhill Castle, Co. Derry, *one of the three large houses built by Frederick Hervey, Earl of Bristol and Bishop of Derry (1730–1803). His passion for building led to the nickname 'The Edifying Bishop'.*

ascribed them to the self-indulgence of a man out of harmony with his time and contemptuously indifferent to what the world might say of him.

The world said a good deal, for such a mass of contradictions could hardly go unremarked: a Bishop who was highly popular in his diocese, and administered its affairs conscientiously, yet who was absent from it for long periods travelling abroad, not returning to it at all during the last eleven years of his life; a man of great religious tolerance, respected by the Roman Catholic and Non-conformist Churches in Ireland, yet a violent partisan liable to extreme personal antipathies; a man commended by Wesley for the reverence with which he conducted services, yet notorious all over Europe for his blasphemous conversation; a man who was 'architecturally hobbied – building is his passion and he indulges it to the highest pitch', yet who spent very little time living in the great houses he had created and never saw his finest creation, Ickworth, at all.

This passion for building, which led the Irish to nickname him 'The Edifying Bishop', was one of the characteristics which seems more eccentric to us, who have to obtain planning permission to erect a potting-shed, than it would have to his contemporaries, many of whom were similarly inclined. It was not the inclination but the lack of restraint with which he indulged it which was thought remarkable. The Earl Bishop built three great houses largely to his own uncon-

41

Augustus Hervey presented by his father to Chatham, *a painting at Ickworth by William Hoare of Bath,
1771. Augustus Hervey was the son of the Earl Bishop.*

ventional design: Downhill and Ballyscullion in Ireland, and Ickworth on the
family estate in Suffolk. But his interests were catholic, and he was also responsible for a large number of church spires, follies, temples, summer-houses and
bridges, including one over the Foyle at Londonderry. He built roads too – The
Bishop's Road over the mountains from Downhill to Strand was described as
'rather the work of a Roman Emperor than an Irish Bishop'. On one occasion,
he asked the wife of one of his clergy, who was in financial difficulties, to stay at
Downhill. She did not like to ask if she could bring her baby, so lodged it in a
nearby village and visited it secretly to feed it. When the Bishop discovered this,
he prudently decided to leave the baby where it was, but 'to facilitate her inter-
course, which was rendered somewhat inconvenient by the badness of the road,

Coat of arms of the Earl Bishop *from the Mussenden Temple at Downhill, a small classical rotunda on the edge of the cliffs built by the Earl Bishop in 1783 as a compliment to his cousin Mrs Mussenden.*

a hundred labourers, in the course of one day, converted a rough and narrow lane into a fine spacious road'.

Of his houses, Downhill was the one he lived in the most. Ickworth and Bally-scullion were built on a similar plan, with an oval central house, flanked by galleries, stables and offices. The Bishop called Ickworth 'an impudent house'. His wife who had a closer acquaintance with it called it 'a stupendous monument of folly'.

Lord Bristol never liked the idea of living at Ickworth because he thought the dampness of the soil injured his health, with which he was much preoccupied. He described his symptoms at length and with relish. 'My last Gout has cleansed the Augean Stable of my Bowels'. Illness he frequently attributed to 'loathed tea, that cursed tea, which unstrings ye all and unfits you for every enjoyment but the flutter for the moment'. He would have done better to look for the cause of his own troubles in his glass rather than his teacup. 'He would drink a bottle of Madeira and swear like a gentleman' . . . but not, one would have hoped, like a bishop.

As a host the Bishop was genial but unpredictable. At Downhill one night after dinner, he pitted his clergy in a series of horse races along the beach against their Non-conformist brethren who, being fitter and less well nourished and accustomed to riding on horseback rather than in a carriage, all won, leaving many of the representatives of the Established Church rolling on the sand, to the Bishop's great amusement. These clerical seaside sports seem to have appealed to him, for on another occasion he made some of the fattest clergy in his diocese run a race on the beach for the prize of a vacant living. As he had set the course across a patch of sinking sands none of them succeeded in reaching the winning-post.

This unsportsmanlike behaviour extended to indoor amusements as well. A lady staying at Downhill was suspected of conducting a liaison with another member of the house-party – but no one knew which one until the Bishop scattered flour on the passage floor outside her room and tracked her down to the guilty bedroom. This was presumably done in a spirit of curiosity, rather than one of moral censure, as he usually looked on such peccadilloes with a lenient eye. Among the Bishop's closest friends were Sir William Hamilton and Emma. One day when he was visiting them in Naples he was closeted with Emma when a lady of very dubious reputation was announced, whereupon the Bishop immediately began to take his leave. When Emma asked why, he observed, 'it is permitted to a Bishop to visit one sinner, but quite unfitting that he should be seen in a brothel'.

The Earl's idiosyncratic taste in dress excited comment wherever he went. He caused consternation in the ranks of the Catholic hierarchy by appearing at services in the Sistine Chapel wearing a rather exotic version of the full dress of an Anglican Bishop. A passer-by in Oxford was once heard to mutter, 'that man cannot be a parson in them there clothes'. On that occasion the Bishop was tastefully attired in 'a light lilac coat, his Volunteer hat, fiercely cocked, laced and with a cockade'. Abroad he flowered out into 'a purple velvet nightcap with a tassel of gold dangling over his shoulder and a sort of mitre to the front; silk stockings and slippers of the same colour, and a short round petticoat . . . fringed with gold. A loose dressing gown of silk was thrown over his shoulders. In this Merry Andrew trim he rode on horseback to the never-ending amusement of all beholders!' The finishing touch was provided by 'a single curl fixed with string to his own short hair'.

His most spectacular appearance was his arrival in Dublin for the Grand Convention of the Volunteers of all Ireland – a body demanding far-reaching reforms, which he espoused with immense enthusiasm. He wore 'a costume half military, half episcopal' and was attended 'by a cortège of young parsons, all

Miniature of the Earl Bishop, *probably painted in Naples during the winter of 1794–95, holding a drawing, perhaps of Ballyscullion. In the background is Vesuvius, which erupted while he was there causing him to be badly injured by a flying rock.*

dashing young fellows and gallantly mounted out of the Bishop's stud, which was the finest in Ireland'. The Bishop, in 'episcopal purple, white gloves with a gold fringe round the wrists and golden tassels and diamond buckles on his knees and shoes, was drawn through the streets in an open Landau by six horses caparisoned with purple ribbons. He never ceased making dignified obeisances to the multitude – "Long Live the Bishop", echoed from every window'.

It was unfortunate that the Bishop chose as his aide in the Volunteer cause a man who was later to be hanged for murder. This was his nephew, known as 'Fighting Fitzgerald', a spirited youth who had recently emerged from prison where he had been confined for abducting his younger brother and shutting his

45

Grand Irish Air Balloon, *an engraving published on 7 October, 1784, alluding to his political activities in Ireland. In the boat are Fox, Burke and North.*

father in a cave with a bear. His friend, Timothy Brecknock, who was eventually hanged with him, spied on the Bishop for the Government. He also had the unsavoury habit of drinking large quantities of his own blood, on the assumption that this would enable him to live until the Millennium. Unfortunately the gallows intervened between him and the proof of his theory.

The Volunteer movement failed, and the Bishop's efforts to influence European politics were even less successful, as his urgent despatches home advising the Government to take various dramatic steps were invariably ignored. He did, however, move in the highest circles at a time when Europe was in ferment, so he was constantly caught up in great events, particularly in Italy and Prussia. He strongly disapproved of the treaty made between France and Prussia, by which Prussia deserted the Allies in favour of neutrality. Soon afterwards at a banquet given by the King of Prussia, the Bishop was offered some capon, which he declined. When the King asked if he disliked the dish – 'Yes, Sire', he replied, 'I have an aversion to all Neutrals'.

Madame Ritz, former mistress of the King of Prussia, was the constant companion of his later years, and he wore her miniature round his neck where one might rather have expected to see a pectoral cross. Other women's names were linked with his after 1782 when he had abruptly left his wife after thirty years of marriage. Poor Lady Bristol; it had been a love match, but in later life the Bishop disapproved of love matches, 'so ominous a lottery, so pregnant with blanks, so improbable a success'. At first he had nicknamed her 'Excellent' or 'Excellent Small'; in later years, always inclined to architectural imagery, he described her as 'a magestick ruin'. He urged his son to a marriage of convenience with the daughter of Frederick William and Madame Ritz – 'I offer a real cornucopia' – and was furious when his son refused to oblige. His ideas on education, thought extremely unconventional by his contemporaries, were many years ahead of his time. He had his son taught 'mathematicks, mechanicks, experimental philosophy . . . the spirit of history, ethics and modern languages – leaving Greek and Latin till we found it necessary'.

This was in line with his own interests which, apart from art and architecture, were largely scientific. He was intensely curious about natural phenomena and was one of the first to discover the connexion between Staffa and the Giant's Causeway. This curiosity nearly cost him his life, when, with misguided enthusiasm, he peered over the rim of Vesuvius when in eruption and was badly injured by a flying rock. His character has been compared to 'a veritable volcano' and volcanoes fascinated him. Perhaps he recognized in himself something of their unpredictable and cruel brilliance.

View of Ballyscullion, Co. Derry, *built by the Earl Bishop. Apart from his three country houses, he was responsible for building a large number of church spires, follies, bridges and roads, one of which was described as 'rather the work of a Roman Emperor than an Irish Bishop'.*

The Bishop's travels were always undertaken with great enthusiasm, whether he was in pursuit of a 'delicious Guido' or a new rock formation. On their early journeys together, his wife wrote home: 'your father is well and *au galop* snuffing every fragrant breeze and exercising himself *tout de bon*'.

He never lost his love of travel for its own sake – which caused him to be known as 'The Nomad Bishop'. It was typical of his restless and changeable character, to which constant novelty was a necessity. Italy, Germany, Switzerland and Austria were his favourite haunts. France he stigmatized as a 'frippery country – a skipping dancing tribe'. Spain he enjoyed, except for the inns, and he even explored such remote areas as Dalmatia. In his old age he planned an expedition

The Church Militant, *an engraving published on 1 June, 1784, showing the Earl Bishop dressed half as an Irish Volunteer and half as a bishop. At the Volunteer Convention in Dublin in November 1783, the Bishop appeared in great pomp as a delegate for Derry attended by a troop of dragoons led by his notorious nephew, 'Fighting Fitzgerald'.*

'with armoured crew, with artists, scholars, etc; and with a kitchen and well-provided cellar', up the Nile to Thebes, but unfortunately Napoleon and the Grand Army got there first.

He describes himself as 'one of the Light cavalry', but this is not borne out by his description of his method of travel. He went on horseback, covering about thirty-five miles a day and sending his baggage ahead, 'geese, turkeys, ducks, shoulders and legs of mutton, preceded by two graduate cooks, masters of arts, who arrive just one hour before us – to find our dinner as ready as our appetites'. He sometimes ran foul of the authorities. In Siena he was eating a bowl of pasta during a religious festival. Maddened, either by the quality of the pasta or by the tinkling of bells below, he threw the bowl out of the window, and the glutinous mass draped itself over the Host, which was being borne in procession past his window. He had to flee the city, and narrowly escaped with his life.

The Bishop's taste as a connoisseur has been much criticized. He did buy a lot of indifferent paintings by contemporary artists living in Italy, but he was a great patron of the Arts. Flaxman, whose sculpture *The Fury of Athamas* is still at Ickworth, was one of his protégés. He was derided at the time because he collected works of the early Masters, whose greatness was then unrecognized – Cimabue, Giotto, Guido da Siena, men whose paintings he described lightly as being 'like many other "trifles" of no use to any but the owner'. His deepest admiration was reserved for Dürer and Rembrandt, and his criticisms of even the greatest Italian Masters could be perverse and dogmatic. 'Michelangelo', he once remarked severely, 'was mad, not sublime.'

It would have pleased this eccentric connoisseur to know that his identification with the Arts persisted even after death. He died in Italy in 1803, but owing to the political situation his body could not be brought home until the following year. It was carried on a British man o'war, whose crew had all the sailor's superstitious dread of a corpse on board. Knowing this, the captain had the Bishop's body packed up in a large crate and shipped to England as 'an antique statue'.

Sir George Sitwell

Sir George was two years old in 1862, when his father died leaving his widow with two young children and an encumbered estate.

Renishaw, the Sitwell home in Derbyshire, was closed down except for a few months in the summer. During one of these visits in his school holidays, Sir George discovered in a lumber-room, a few old chests filled with papers. There were bundles of old letters falling into dust, tradesmen's bills from Queen Anne's reign, almanacs bound in leather and tied with silk strings, inventories and household books. Here the everyday lives of the Sacheverells and Sitwells from the fifteenth century onwards lay forgotten.

The records of Sir George's life might easily have joined those of his forbears. His own literary works, *A brief history of Weston Hall, Northamptonshire and of the families that possessed it*, or *The Barons of Pulford in the eleventh and twelfth centuries and their descendants*, for example, although scholarly researched and thorough, were not of the stuff to shake off lumber-room dust.

However, it did not suit his three remarkable and formidable children, Edith, Osbert and Sacheverell, to be sired by a country squire with a taste for genealogy. If Dame Edith and Sir Osbert could not, like Athene, spring fully armed from Jupiter's head, or be born from the spray of the sea like Aphrodite, something must be made of Sir George. In their autobiographies, they pick out and polish his singularities. Dame Edith's visual impression of him in *Taken Care Of* is that 'with his strange, pale, wild, lonely-looking eyes, and his red beard, he resembled a portrait of one of the Borgias or some other early Italian tyrant'.

His appearance and his behaviour provided good material for their prose to embellish. Where they were self-consciously original, he was naturally so. He was a poised listener, at some point outside time, feeling himself as at home in Eckington in the thirteenth century as in his own century, or indeed in H. G. Wells' *The Time Machine*, in which he took a particular interest. He would as a result occasionally get a little muddled as to which century he was listening to, or intermix part of one with another.

In 1876 when he was sixteen, Florence, his sister, writes in her diary, 'In the afternoon I sat out in the garden with Mother, while George went to be photo-

51

Sir George Sitwell (1860–1943), *a lithograph by Vincent Brooks, Day and Son Ltd. Dame Edith Sitwell, Sir George's daughter, said of him: 'with his strange, pale, wild, lonely-looking eyes, and his red beard, he resembled a portrait of one of the Borgias or some other early Italian tyrant'.*

graphed in a suit of armour by Canon Harford.' He was fond of finding reasons to don his armour. In later life, when Lord Macaulay described the country squire in Charles II's reign as a gross, uneducated, untravelled gentleman with the deportment, the vocabulary and the accent of a carter, he felt as insulted as if there had been no time-lapse of two hundred years between the lifetime of Lord Macaulay's squire and his own. He took up the gauntlet with a bristling defence of the Tory squires 'upon whose memory Lord Macaulay has heaped the coarsest epithets of a not very refined vocabulary, the falsest coin of a not very sterling rhetoric'. Lord Macaulay must have been amazed to meet such pugilism on a subject so obscure.

Sir George had particular difficulty in remembering to adjust to the changing scale of money values over the years. His mother's careful and astute handling of the family finances during his minority meant that he was not impoverished. He spent long hours poring over old household accounts. He found that in the 1660s 'Wax candles for the Hall were procured from George Halbersley, a chandler in the village, at the cost of four or five shilling a dozen; soap in the form of washing balls was manufactured at the farm at the cost of a shilling a dozen and about 52 dozen represent the annual consumption'.

He would emerge from these absorbing calculations and astonish his family and their friends by his wildly disproportionate extremes of extravagance and meanness. He took on four thousand unemployed constituents from Scarborough to create a lake at Renishaw. He thought nothing of having full-grown yew trees raised or lowered in order to alter a view. He planned glass fountains and stone serpents for the lake. He even had his whole herd of white cattle stencilled in a blue Chinese pattern, presumably to their great discomfort. Labour, after all, cost little in the seventeenth century from which he had just been disturbed.

Visitors to Renishaw, however, were bewildered to find that while their host was indulgent to his own every whim in matters of architecture or landscape, he only provided two candles apiece to light their enormous ghostly bedrooms. There was no electric light at Renishaw until after he died. Sir Osbert describes him with delight, writing in 1915 to tell Sacheverell's house-master at Eton that as he had been particularly hard hit by the War he would pay the term's school fees in pigs and potatoes instead of cash.

As he felt himself to be an observer of life rather than a participant, he had no idea that either his behaviour or his appearance could in any way affect anybody else. Constant Lambert, eating a solitary breakfast at Renishaw, was more than a little disturbed to see Sir George passing the window on all fours with his cane clenched between his teeth. He was considering dropping the lawn by three feet

Renishaw Hall, Derbyshire, *the seat of the Sitwells, after a drawing by Rex Whistler. It was here that Sir George had his whole herd of white cattle stencilled in a blue Chinese pattern.*

and quite practically wished to observe the view from the new level. He was equally unaware that anybody would find anything amusing about his habit of carrying a rubber air-cushion everywhere he went. This complete self-isolation, this inability to understand that other people had more thoughts or feelings than marbles in a game of Solitaire, had tragic as well as comic consequences.

54

ABOVE: Sir George at Montegufoni in 1935, *a photograph from a family album. He bought the Castle of Montegufoni in 1909 and he and Lady Ida lived there almost permanently after 1926.*
BELOW: Sir George, his sister Florence and their mother, *after a drawing by George du Maurier. Sir George inherited the baronetcy at the age of two.*

The Sitwell Family by John Singer Sargent (1856–1925). Painted at Renishaw, the Sitwell family home, in 1900, this delightful family portrait shows Sir George and his beautiful but spendthrift wife Lady Ida together with their children Edith, Osbert and Sacheverell.

He married in 1886 Lady Ida, daughter of the Earl of Londesborough, when she was seventeen. She was very beautiful. Du Maurier drew her as the Duchess of Towers in his illustrations to *Peter Ibbetson*. Sir George felt utterly alien to the frivolous and empty-headed woman he considered her to be, and drew himself

56

as far away as possible from any intimacy their close relationship might force on him. His wife was incapable of understanding the complexity of his character. She found him strange, aloof and disdainful, and she was frightened of him.

She was by nature gay and extravagant. Sir George paid her debts with increasing irritation until in 1911 she found that she had exhausted his store of patience and her own resources and still owed £2,000. At this point she was by ill luck introduced to a moneylender called Julian Field, who unscrupulously took advantage of her complete ignorance of financial affairs. Lady Ida signed the documents he gave her and claimed that any letters she wrote thereafter were fair copies drafted by Field. The ghastly culmination came on 9 March, 1915, when Lady Ida, Julian Field and one Oliver Herbert appeared before the Central Criminal Court charged with conspiring together to cheat and defraud a certain Frances Dobbs and to fraudulently induce her to accept certain bills of change.

Julian Field had badly miscalculated. He had assumed throughout that when Sir George realized the position his wife was in, he would settle any amount of debts (by this time she had signed papers which made her responsible for £30,000) rather than expose her and her family to the degradation of a lawsuit. He did not realize the extent of Lady Ida's fear of her husband, which made her conceal what she was doing from him and destroy letters sent to him until she was so deeply entangled that the first of the series of lawsuits that preceded the Crown prosecution was imminent. Least of all did he imagine that when Sir George finally did find out, he would refuse to pay.

As Sir George saw it, from his principled pinnacle, the only way to make Field harmless to other potential victims was to expose him, even if it involved his wife appearing in court. He refused to budge from this position until it was too late and the series of lawsuits had turned into the inexorable reality of a Crown prosecution from which even he could not escape. He appeared in the witness box on 15 March, 1915. Later the same day, both his wife and Julian Field were found guilty.

It was the black climax to four years of intermittent fear and anguish for the whole family. No tower or portcullis or drawbridge could protect Sir George from this ugly and sordid encounter with reality. He wrote, much later, in 1933, 'the marking down of singularity as a branch of vain-glory, of debt as a state of bondage as generous as deadly sin, deserves consideration, and without doubt self-knowledge will have been gained by those who listened to it'. He was writing about Christian teaching in Chaucer's time, but his mind must also have been on his own experience.

By 1915 his time of public service was over. He had twice been Member of

Sir George in 1935, *a photograph from the album of his grandson, Reresby Sitwell.*

The Castle of Montegufoni. *Sir George installed in one room a beautiful sixteenth-century gold bed on which appears a rose, inspired by the Papal Golden Rose awarded to ladies of 'tried virtue'. At the age of sixteen he was photographed in a suit of armour and, pursuing the same interest, he re-equipped the armoury at Montegufoni.*

Parliament for Scarborough and also High Sheriff of Derbyshire. His best literary work, *On the Making of Gardens*, had been received with only moderate enthusiasm. He was fifty-three, when a man might allow himself to mellow a little. Sir George, however, redoubled his private battle with life and his energy increased proportionately.

He travelled to and from Italy, where he had bought the Castle of Montegufoni in 1909, accompanied, when they were on speaking terms, by his servant, Henry

59

Moat, whom he referred to as 'The Great Man'. He brought back quantities of objects for Renishaw and Wood End, the house in Scarborough. On one trip he discovered two altar-vases that he thought would convert into handy paraffin lamps.

In between voyages he attacked his literary tasks in one of his seven studies at Renishaw, or in the Reading Room at the British Museum. His customary detachment led to an almost unbearably exact sense of proportion. 'The race was healthy', he wrote of the medieval English, 'a high infantile death-rate ensuring the disappearance with little physical or mental suffering of those weakly strains which we take so much trouble to perpetuate'. And in the preface to his next published work, a slim volume whimsically entitled *Idle fancies in prose and verse*, he promises that as an antidote to the melancholy of his verses he will add a postscript on the forward march of science.

Meanwhile his children found in his spare time his interest in themselves had increased alarmingly. Vigorous as they were, they felt totally overpowered by it. When they were under the same roof, he would bombard them with unsolicited advice, condemnation and rhetorical consultation. If they were elsewhere, he would continue the daily barrage by post. In self-defence Osbert had managed to persuade his parents to emigrate to Montegufoni in 1925, although they made frequent trips back to England.

Sir George lived on until he was eighty-three, to his surprise. He had always thought he would die young. Lady Ida died in 1937. Henry Moat, who had retired the year before, commented lugubriously that at least Sir George would now know where her Ladyship spent her afternoons.

When Italy declared war on England in 1940, Sir George was at Montegufoni. While those of his compatriots still in Italy struggled to get out, he stayed on in his castle, his 'Fancy Tower'.

> IN FANCY'S tower, the lattice high
> Looks proudly out on earth and sky.
>
> As in a mirror one may spy
> The world's great pageant rolling by,
> Or, turning to the past, may know
> The lives that men lived long ago.
> A scytheless Time sets back the hour
> In Fancy's tower.

He died three years later, in Switzerland. He left a small English estate, of about £10,000. His will ran to seventeen pages, with three codicils.

Mary Kingsley

Mary Kingsley was scarcely exceptional in appearance in her stout Victorian skirt and prim head-dress, the umbrella with which she prodded hippopotami and took marine soundings, but all these seem to identify her with the conventionally unconventional sisterhood of other Victorian lady travellers. She shares with them also a kind of innocent valour which carried her round many tight corners and allowed her to come pretty close to pitch without defilement. But the quality of her intellect was unique, her political judgment on African affairs strikingly ahead of her times; her opinions, founded on rational thinking, were her own and little influenced by current fashion.

The 'Scramble for Africa' was at its height in 1893 when Mary Kingsley, released at the age of thirty from a lifetime of devoted attendance on her parents, strode on board a Liverpool cargo-boat, bound for West Africa, her luggage consisting of a portmanteau, a black bag and 'a waterproof sack neatly closed at the top with a bar and handle', packed with blankets, boots and books. She inherited a passion for travel and an unquenchable vitality from her father, a younger brother of the more famous Charles. George Kingsley was a restless, eccentric man who read much and travelled widely, leaving his wife in England, often anxious and always lonely, to bring up Mary and her brother Charles in various homes, of which the last was at Cambridge.

Mary was born on 13 October, 1862. She was largely self-taught with a taste for science and an aptitude for the practical application of knowledge; a course in German was the only part of her education which cost her father a penny. When her parents died within a few weeks of each other, she was left suddenly with no purpose in life; she determined to try and complete her father's unfinished work on native religions. West Africa was her chosen field of research and scientific friends suggested that while there she should study and collect freshwater fish and other zoological specimens – 'fish and fetish' is how she described her objects in going to 'skylark and enjoy myself in Africa'. The slangy phrases are as typical of her style in speech and writing, as they are unexpressive of the deep seriousness of her mind, sometimes verging on melancholy, and of her exceptional integrity.

In the short interval between August 1893 and November 1895, Mary Kingsley

Mary Kingsley (1862–1900), *a signed photograph with the inscription in her writing, 'the melancholy picture of one who tried to be just to all parties', the portrait of a determined and independent Victorian 'voyager'.*

was to become famous as a traveller in the grand tradition of Livingstone. Her education as a 'coaster' began on the voyage out, when her fellow passengers, West Coast traders to a man, entertained her with stories – dismal, macabre and comic – of the dangers and discomforts of the 'white man's grave'. They took her for a missionary with her drab clothes, gaunt figure and scraped-back hair, but were undeceived by her 'failure during a Sunday service in the Bay of Biscay, to rescue it from the dire confusion into which it had been thrown by an esteemed and able officer and a dutiful but inexperienced purser'. An agnostic, and unsympathetic to missions, Mary had determined to travel as a trader, feeling that thus could she best gain the confidence of the bush Africans whose ways she had come to study. She carried the usual trade goods, principally cloth and tobacco, to exchange for ivory and rubber, and was accredited to the West Coast firm of Hatton and Cookson; nothing if not resourceful, she once traded twelve of her own 'ladies' blouses' to get herself out of a dangerous spot, and noted with interest their effect 'when worn by a brawny warrior with *nothing* else but red paint and a bunch of leopard tails'.

On her first journey, she landed at St Paul de Loanda and travelled north through the Congo Free State, into the French Congo and so to Old Calabar. She returned with a valuable collection of natural-history specimens, a working knowledge of trade English (the lingua franca of the Coast) and an immense respect for the traders, white and black, in out-of-the-way places who had made her so welcome. She learnt to travel rough, living off the country on unappetizing 'native chop', and at different times, then and later, she learnt about ships – how to handle them and live in them, how to stow cargo and how to manage a native crew.

She embarked for her second journey, again from Liverpool, in 1894, accompanying Lady MacDonald whose husband was governor of Calabar. She stayed there for five months, collecting fish and insects and indulging her insatiable appetite for water and mud by paddling through the mangrove swamps of the Oil Rivers, beset by flies and crocodiles. From Calabar she visited that redoubtable missionary Mary Slessor, from whom she learnt much about native ways, though without modifying her own general attitude to mission Christianity.

The really exciting phase of Mary Kingsley's adventures began when she left Calabar bound for the upper reaches of the Ogowé in the French Congo. Laden with trade goods, and with introductions to French mission stations (she gave a qualified approval to the French Evangelicals), she established a base near Lambarene, of Albert Schweitzer fame, and made a daring sally by canoe up the Ogowé. Rapid after rapid was surmounted, the African crew alternately singing

Natives of Gabon, *a photograph published in 'Travels in West Africa' by Mary Kingsley, 1897. In the villages she visited she doctored the inhabitants in traditional style, took part in legal palavers and studied the local customs. Her one indulgence on her travels was endless cups of tea.*

hymns and yelling 'Jump for bank, sar!' when the water became too rough. 'One appalling corner I shall not forget, for I had to jump at a rock wall, and hang on to it in a manner more befitting an insect than an insect-hunter'. Back from this trip, her appetite whetted for better acquaintance with the savage Fans met for the first time in up-river villages, she projected an even more dangerous journey. Striking north from the Ogowé, with only five African companions, she aimed to cut through almost unexplored bush and reach Gabon across country and by way of the Rembwé River. They picked up four Fans at the first village they came to, bold buccaneering spirits who delighted Miss Kingsley and terrified her men. Kiva was 'a born hunter'; Wiki, skilled in bushcraft, took the lead in hauling her out of a wild-beast trap in which she might have been fatally impaled but for her good thick skirt; Fika was simply 'a fine young fellow'. The fourth member of the party, 'A Fan gentleman with the manners of a duke and the habits of a dustbin', came uninvited 'to see the fun, and drop in for a fight if there was one going on'. It was 'the Duke' who suggested that Mary should go ahead into a doubtful village to test the probable hostility of the natives, an assignment she declined with unruffled good humour, observing, 'There's nothing like dash and courage, my dear Duke, even if one displays it by deputy, so this plan of yours does you great credit . . .' But she always took her turn in leading over swampy ground, sometimes going in up to her neck. She taught the Fans English, throwing in for good measure (or, in trade English, 'a dash for top') such expressions as 'Stuff, my dear Sir!' and 'Dear me now!' They pressed on through forest and swamp, menaced by gorillas, snakes and cannibals; all was grist to Mary's mill, even when she failed to follow the advice of a 'valued scientific friend': 'Always take measurements, Miss Kingsley, and always take them from the adult male'. Best of all she enjoyed the sojourns at Fan villages where she doctored the inhabitants in traditional style, took part in legal palavers and studied the local customs. Danger simmered just below the surface, adding a zest to the exercise, a flavour to the endless cups of tea which were her one indulgence. Awaking one night to a strange smell, she located some grisly human remains hanging in a bag over her bed; calmly tipping into her hat ('for fear of losing anything of value') a shrivelled hand, some toes, eyes and ears, she registered in her notebook the Fan custom of keeping 'mementoes' of their victims. Was this hat the pillbox which is the pride of the Royal Geographical Society's Museum?

Mary Kingsley's hat, *perhaps the receptacle for some human remains – a shrivelled hand, some toes, eyes and ears – which she once found hanging over her bed and which, for scientific reasons, she tipped into her hat and preserved.*

At the Rembwé she paid off her men in trade goods from Hatton and Cookson's bush store and came down the river in spanking style with an African trader called Obanjo – 'but he liked it pronounced Captain Johnson'. 'There was a Hallo-my-Hearty atmosphere coming off him from the top of his hat to the soles of his feet, like the scent of a flower'. From Gabon she visited Corisco Island on an abortive quest for rare fish, and on her way back to England landed in the German Cameroons and achieved the ascent of the Cameroon Mountain from the difficult landward side. Arriving, *en route*, soaked to the skin and her skirt

Mary Kingsley's canoe on the Ogowé River. *It was on this part of her journey that she was forced to jump at a rock wall and hang on to it 'in a manner more befitting an insect than an insect-hunter'.*

caked with mud, at a German outpost of civilization, Victorian inhibitions re-asserted themselves and she indignantly refused a hot bath because of the 'very sketchy wooden window shutters'.

In the five years after her return Mary Kingsley became acknowledged as an expert on all things West African – on the customs of the natives and the re-sponsibilities of their white rulers. She championed two unpopular causes: she thought the traders rather than the missionaries were the real heroes of the Guinea coast, and she advocated a deeper understanding and tolerance of African religious and legal forms than was then thought allowable. Her campaign for a just and practical administration of Britain's newly acquired territories in West Africa brought her fame, but it prevented her from travelling again. In addition to lecturing and much other writing she published two classics of African travel. *Travels in West Africa* (1897) she described as a 'word swamp of a book', and so it is, if we remember that to Mary Kingsley swamps were beautiful, unpredictable and productive of much comic incident. 'The voyager', as she calls herself in the chapter-headings, recalls moments of rapture, in the moonlight of the 'foaming, flying Ogowé', perhaps, or with mist swirling round her head in a lonely forest clearing. She takes the reader scudding down the Rembwé at the tiller of Captain Johnson's boat, a counterpane for a sail. There is plenty of custard-pie stuff, and some quaint musings: were the hippos the first or last of creatures? Had 'Nature's prentice hand' perpetrated them, or had she tired of beautiful creations and exclaimed at last: 'Here, just put these other viscera into big bags – I can't bother any more'. *West African Studies* (1899) is also full of good things, and in both there is much solid information on 'fish and fetish'.

In 1900 she volunteered for service in South Africa, and died nursing Boer prisoners at Simonstown on 3 June, 1900. By her own last wish she was buried at sea, a voyager to the end.

Sir Tatton Sykes

On hearing of the death of Sir Tatton Sykes, the famous 'Auld Squire' of York-shire, an old East Yorkshire farmer-sportsman remarked: 'Aye, whya, there may be manny mair Sir Tatton Sykeses, but there'll nivver be another Sir Tatton'. He was echoing the reverence akin to idolatry which the people of Yorkshire had held for 'The 'Auld Squire', and when in 1863, following his father's death, the second Sir Tatton took the baronetcy, he was under no illusions about what he had to compete with.

Tatton's father had done little to inspire confidence in his sons, once remarking that while his son Christopher was 'only good for helping ladies out of carriages', Tatton was 'good for nowt', He had taken little interest in him as a child, often behaving in a cruel and tyrannical way, and as soon as he was old enough, the young Tatton was, in effect, driven abroad, where he travelled extensively for many years. It is hardly surprising that when the news of his father's death was brought to him, his only reaction was to repeat again and again 'Oh! Indeed!'

Tatton's relationship with his parents caused him great unhappiness, and much of the eccentricity for which he became known may well have been attributable to his state of mind. While he hated his father, he adored his mother. She, how-ever, had little time for her son, preferring to spend her time at Sledmere, enjoying the pleasures of gardening in the splendid orangery that stood in the grounds, or among the numerous hothouses. Her passion for flowers even extended to her giving seeds to the villagers to sow in their front gardens. The rest of the time she spent away in London, enjoying her social life.

Tatton resented his mother's lack of interest deeply, and this may well have been the reason for his eccentric obsession about flowers, which started with the deliber-ate destruction of the beautiful gardens as one of his first acts on taking over at Sledmere. The orangery was demolished; the hothouses were dismantled; not even the lawns were left intact, for, giving the excuse that the grass needed 'turn-ing' to make it grow better, he had them all ploughed up, right to the dining-room window.

The cultivation of flowers was strictly forbidden for, as he once told his daughter-in-law, who was trying to explain how much pleasure flowers gave to the

Spy cartoon of Sir Tatton Sykes, *of Sledmere, the squire with a hatred of flowers and gossiping women.*

women in the village, he considered them to be 'nasty, untidy things'. On many an occasion, Sir Tatton could be seen making a tour of inspection in the village, his walking-stick ready to slash the heads off any unsuspecting plants he might come upon. To the distressed cottager who emerged in time to witness a whirl of flying petals, he would declare: 'If you wish to grow flowers, grow cauliflowers!'

So strongly did he insist upon his views that in time the old-fashioned 'posies' disappeared from the Sledmere Estate, though one of his tenants, who was never converted from roses to vegetables, plainly told Sir Tatton on one occasion: 'Whya, it's this way: if you tak t'flooers, you'll 'a'e ti tak my auld woman ez weel'.

Cold, flowerless and without a woman since 1861, when his mother had died, Sledmere must have seemed a bleak place to the young wife that Sir Tatton brought home with him in 1874. She was Jessica Cavendish-Bentinck, and they had met in Germany where she was travelling with her mother, Penelope Leslie. Known as 'Britannia', Penelope Leslie was a formidable woman who pushed her daughter into the marriage. At the age of eighteen, Jessica was thirty years Tatton's junior and, in the light of this and his extraordinary character, it is hardly surprising that it was a disaster.

Tatton's routine at Sledmere was not exactly designed to keep a young wife happy. When once asked to what he attributed his long life, Sir Tatton replied: 'To going to bed early, getting up early, and treating my stomach with respect'. This meant that he would be out walking in the park each morning by six o'clock. As for treating his stomach with respect, he insisted on eating milk puddings wherever he went, even when staying at the Grand Metropole Hotel in London. To ensure a good milk pudding he used to take his own cook, Mrs Pember, to the hotel with him and there, each day, she would be mortally embarrassed as she prepared her strange dish, surrounded by laughing French chefs.

In the 1870s and early '80s Tatton and Jessica managed to live fairly amicably together. She took up writing and completed several novels, while Tatton busied himself with the work for which he was to become famous. With his nephew, Henry Cholmondeley, he vastly improved the stud which his father had started, refining it down to a smaller and much better unit.

With the brilliant architect, Mr Temple More, he built and restored churches all over the East Riding, expending a sum of over a million and a half pounds on the work. He once told his son, Mark, that in his early travels he had been hugely impressed by the great number of people making pilgrimages to the holy cities and by all the crosses and memorials that had been built along the roads as a reminder of these journeys. He had thought then, he said, what a great shame it was that there was nothing similar in the East Riding of Yorkshire, no demonstration

69

The fire at Sledmere, a photograph taken on 23 May, 1911. When advised to leave the burning house, Sir Tatton said, 'First I must finish my pudding, finish my pudding' – perhaps the milk pudding he had to have prepared for him wherever he went. Sir Tatton is in the foreground wearing a trilby.

of the faith of the people.

His work with Temple More enabled him to indulge his one great romantic fantasy: to see himself as one of the last corner stones of the Gothic Revival and, at the dedication of one of his last works, the restoration of the ancient church of St Hilda's at Sherburn-in-the-Forest, the Archbishop of York said, 'there will always remain for him, among the Wolds and plains of this part of Yorkshire, a memorial which time itself will not be able to efface – churches which, by his love and reverence, he has restored to the beauty which once adorned them in the days gone by'.

By the mid-1880s the relationship between Tatton and Jessica began to deteriorate rapidly, with Jessica turning to drink and heavy gambling for consolation, while Tatton retired more and more into himself, his eccentricity all the while increasing. He strongly maintained the theory that in order to remain in the best possible health, a person should attempt to keep his body at a constant temperature. Owing to his having spent so much time in the East, Sir Tatton favoured an Oriental temperature and therefore became accustomed to wearing six overcoats which he would discard, one at a time, as his body temperature rose, a sight that was recalled by one of the Sledmere villagers who said of him: 'When he was here, after coming back from abroad, he would have a lot of coats on and, as the day got warmer, he used to take them off, roll them up, and place them any-where, where ever he was, and us lads we knew that if we took the coats back to the butler we would get a shilling'. Once, when he made a rare trip to Ascot races where, amongst all the gentry in their finery, he must have looked a very odd sight, his brother, Christopher was mortally embarrassed when the then Prince of Wales, Edward VII, turned to him and, pointing at Tatton, asked: 'Who is that extraordinary looking man over there? Why on earth do they allow people in the enclosure dressed in such ridiculous clothes?'

Newspaper cutting of 1897 *referring to the trial of Sir Tatton versus his wife: Sykes versus Sykes. He is described here as* 'a man of helpless eccentricity' *and* 'an obstinate and extremely whimsical old gentleman'.

the less easy to remove, because there are certain technical difficulties in the way of a direct prosecution for forgery. On the other hand, her husband is presented to us as a man of helpless eccentricity, utterly unable to make any rational use of his vast wealth. His appearance in the box was pitiful. The main charge made by the witnesses against him, namely that he was a vacillating and ridiculous person, whose memory could not be relied on, was largely corroborated by his own exhibition in the character of a witness. He dealt with the Court and the opposing counsel in a way which suggests that he must be a very difficult person to deal with in private life. The judge described him as " an obstinate and extremely whimsical old gentleman," and the epithets are not extravagant. As to the household affairs, the evidence is in conflict, and there is no reason why we should seek to unravel the mystery. Lady Sykes declared that this curious millionaire

Photograph of Sir Tatton Sykes at Sledmere, *where he died on 4 May, 1913.*

Portrait of Lady Sykes, *born Jessica Cavendish-Bentinck, wife of Sir Tatton.*

Sometimes, along with the overcoats, he would even wear two pairs of trousers and on one occasion, when on York Station with his son Mark and a friend, he proceeded, in full view of all, to remove a pair. There was nothing indecent about it, of course, because he was wearing another pair underneath, but neither Mark nor his friend knew this and were, therefore, deeply embarrassed. Another time, when he got too hot sitting in a train, he simply removed his shoes and socks and stuck his feet out of the window.

Sir Tatton had other strange obsessions, too, one of which was an intense dislike of cottagers on the Estate using their front doors. In order to prevent this, he insisted that all the existing doors were locked, barred and bolted, and some cottages were even built with false front doors. Various reasons have been suggested for this manifestation of his eccentricity. Some said that he hated to see women gossiping and that, as he thought it was impossible to prevent them doing so, he would compel them not to gossip on their doorsteps. Another theory was that he hated to see children running about in the village street, and that he wished to restrict them to playing in their backyards. This seems to be borne out by a contemporary of Sir Tatton who wrote: 'On one of my visits some building was going on. As children will, they loved to play around amongst the bricks, etc. Sir Tatton said to the foreman: "Now if those children come all bothering round, I'll turn all their parents out of their cottages"'.

Yet along with this occasional sternness and severity, Tatton was capable of humour and had a way of mixing with his tenants that endeared him to them. He could speak the Yorkshire dialect like a native, and loved to drop into their expressive colloquial speech when chatting with farmers, as this story, told by a Malton pig-dealer, shows:

I had managed to buy some pork pigs off Mr Gill, Sir Tatton's farm bailiff, and was to be at the home farm with my cart at 2.00 pm. When I got there I saw an old man with a scarf round his neck, an old slouch hat on, and a suit I wouldn't have given five shillings for, wandering about the yard. I went with the old man and had a look at the pigs – a grand lot. He said: 'What's ta think they'll be worth?' I replied: 'Whya noo, they're aboot nine stone apiece, I should think'. 'Aye' says he, 'what's ta going ti bid Gill when he cums, mi lad?' 'Oh' I said, 'Ah'll give him forty-five shillings, they're worth it. But "Oad Tat" has heaps o' money, an' Ah sahn't bid him na mair nor forty shillings at t'outside – less 'an that if Ah can mannish it. Ah can tell ya, maister, Ah's nut sa green as you think!' Then Gill came and I heard 'im and t'oad man muttering an' talking. Then t'oad man laughed and Gill said 'Oh, I shouldn't let 'im have 'em Sir Tatton!' Well, a feather wad 'ae felled me. T'oad fellow tht Ah'd been talking 'teea had been Sir Tatton himself.

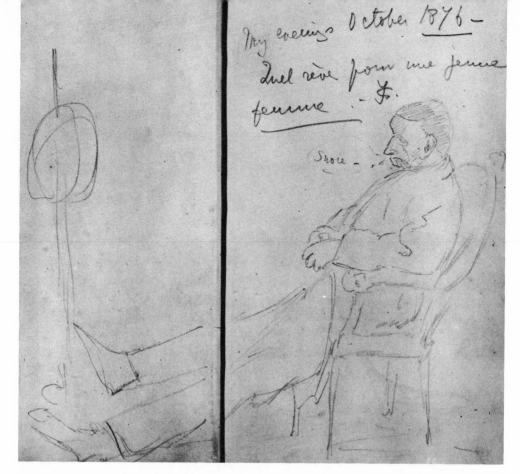

Pencil Sketch in the front of a bound, hand-written book entitled 'Margiana' by Jessica Sykes. It depicts Sir Tatton asleep in a chair and snoring, and the inscription suggests Jessica's discontent as a young wife.

By the late 1890s, Jessica's behaviour had become intolerable to Tatton, for while he was naturally reclusive and spent most of his time at Sledmere upstairs in his rooms, she lived in a fashionable whirl of drinking and gambling, and her debts were becoming formidable. Then, in 1896, a law was passed which said that a man could become legally free of his wife's debts if he openly published in a newspaper that he no longer considered himself responsible. In 1897 Sir Tatton became the first man to take this step, and there followed what proved to be a sensational and sad round of trials: Sykes versus Sykes.

Jessica claimed that she had been driven to do what she had by Tatton's extreme meanness, and she told the court that he suffered from incipient insanity, quoting the story of the overcoats as an example. Ripples of laughter filled the courtroom as she attempted to ridicule her husband. The truth of the matter was that Jessica was a heavy gambler, not only at the tables, but also in finance, and she had lost a sum of which the modern equivalent would be close on one million pounds. Tatton was made to take the stand and, because he was getting old and his memory was beginning to fail, he found himself in a position where he actually had to defend himself. In the end he won the case, but only at the cost of exposing his eccentricities to public ridicule.

The Death of Sir Tatton Sykes

Hark; Hark; tis the death-bell's toll
Too true, the Baronet's dead,
Hes had His last, long, long, sleep
His last words have been said.

His voice is stilled, yea, stilled for aye
His face no more we see,
His kindly eyes are closed in death.
For all eternity.

His name will live, yea, live for aye
T'will live right through the ages,
Sir Tatton's name can never die
T'will live in history's pages.

T'will live, t'will live in worker's homes
A friend of workers ever,
He recognised the worker's lot
A worker slight Him, never.

T'will live in church, t'will live in school
In town and Hamlet too,
When other names are dead, t'will be
As fresh, as mornings dew.

The Curtain's drawn, the head is bowed
The Flag flies but half mast,
Sorrow has come to every Home.
Yea, more than a gloom's being cast.

To Him, to Him, who gave that life
That life, it hath returned,
Thou Good, and Faithful servant go
And take, Thy rest, well earned.

Eddlethorpe May 1913.   S. Watson.

Poem on the death of Sir Tatton, *probably composed by one of his retainers.*

The closing years of Sir Tatton's life were further saddened by the almost complete destruction of Sledmere by fire on 23 May, 1911. It started in a smouldering beam that protruded into the kitchen chimney and worked its way into the roof. Sir Tatton was eating his lunch when he was told the news, and was advised to leave the house. 'First,' he said, 'I must finish my pudding, finish my pudding'. After he had done so he sat on a chair in front of the house and watched his home being gradually destroyed. An eyewitness wrote: 'To the eye of a connoisseur it was a heart-rending sight, and to the owner, a solitary figure amidst it all, watching the tongues of fire pursuing their destructive course, it must have caused many a pang of inward regret. Yet all he said, when a word of sympathy was offered, was: '"These things will happen, these things will happen!" repeating the words with resigned fortitude and recognizing the utter hopelessness of it all'.

Soon after this, and the death of Jessica in 1912, he became convinced that at 11.30 one morning he was going to die. Each morning his mount, an old cob, was brought round for him to ride. Some days he would go out while, on others, he would send his groom away, saying 'No, no, can't ride, can't ride, going to die, going to die!' In fact it was at 3.00 am on 4 May, 1913, that he finally passed away, after suffering a bad attack of pneumonia that had lasted three weeks.

In retrospect, eccentricity is almost always funny, and eccentrics have been the source of many an amusing tale. The reality, however, is often different, for much of their behaviour must have been very difficult to cope with. With Sir Tatton this was certainly true of his destruction of flowers, his hatred of children and his dictatorial edicts forbidding villagers to be seen at their front doors. The other side of his eccentricity was quite harmless; that of taking commonsense to its extreme logical limits – if you wanted to be at the same temperature and were wearing two pairs of trousers, then it was very wise to remove one pair. Whatever can be said of his peculiarities, they marked out Sir Tatton as a true character and for this, and the great legacy he left behind in the stud and his magnificent churches, he will always be remembered in the East Riding of Yorkshire.

Thomas de Quincey

Thomas de Quincey, the opium-eater, contemporary of Coleridge, Wordsworth and Keats, was to his generation a puzzle, a paradox and an eternal source of bewilderment. His uniqueness may have been intensified by his addiction to opium, but this in turn was a symptom of those rare qualities which were deeply inherent in him even as a child and which made him an eccentric man of genius.

Hill Burton in *The Bookhunter* writes of De Quincey in his description of Papaverius: 'The next slide of the lantern is to represent a quite peculiar and abnormal case. It introduces a strangely fragile, unsubstantial and puerile figure, wherein, however, resided one of the most potent and original spirits that ever frequented a tenement of clay'. His eyes were dark in colour, but had a strange flatness and dimness of aspect; his face from a distance appeared hale and smooth, but when closely examined it was as if one million wrinkles crossing in every direction had been drawn by the point of a very fine needle. He appeared old when he was still young with 'his arched brow loaded with thought', but when in conversation, we are told by a friend, 'strange light beamed from that grief-worn face, and for a little while that weak body, so long fed upon by pain, seemed to be clothed with supernatural youth'. His voice was extraordinary: it came as if from dreamland; but it was the most musical of voices, used in a tone of sustained melody.

Vast as were his attainments, and various as were his acute perception of human character and motivation, his nonchalant demeanour, his mirth and fervent eloquence, there was an underlying lack of healthy balance in his mental faculties. His imagination was abnormally active so that in spite of solid intellectual powers, his reason could easily be dominated. It was as if the incidents of his everyday life were too disturbing to him and he had to transform events and surroundings into objects of pleasure by detaching them from disagreeable circumstances.

Throughout De Quincey's life, visions and dreams, abstract thoughts and events seem to have intermingled and become diffused so that very often fantasy and reality could not be disentangled. When he was only six years old, Elizabeth, his favourite eldest sister, who was his 'gentlest and most beloved companion',

Very truly yours,
Thomas de Quincey

Thomas de Quincey (1785–1859), *a portrait of the author in middle age, with his signature. His clothes were threadbare and he wore fragments of apparel that were nearest to hand when he dressed: 'Those not accustomed to eccentric habits got the impression of poverty'. His face was worn with grief from an early age and marked by opium-taking.*

De Quincey manuscript, an extract of 1848 describing the torture of abstinence from the drug. In that year he succeeded in finding the minimum dose that made existence endurable.

died on a bright midsummer day. When all was quiet and the family away, he surreptitiously entered the bedchamber where her little corpse lay, and as he watched her face 'of noble intellectual promise', he entered into a trance and in the flood of sunshine that streamed from the cloudless sky outside, he felt as if a 'wind that might have swept the fields of mortality for a thousand centuries' was rising and swelling till the eye partook of the magic of the ear. Her image from then on was to dwell with him, and she represented a visionary guard from the spiritual world.

A similar influence was effected by Ann, the Oxford Street prostitute he met while he was living in abject poverty in London, having run away from Manchester Grammar School. At eighteen his scholarship in Greek and Latin was infinitely

Opium poppy (Papaver somniferum), *the source of both his happiness and his despair. He became an expert in the effects of opium, revealing in 'Confessions of an English Opium-eater' the extent of opium-taking in England in the early nineteenth century when it could be purchased quite easily and for a few pence.*

superior to that of his teachers, and the sense of futility of a life spent below his intellectual level, the loneliness of a personality so different and alien from his school contemporaries, compelled him to set off alone and without money. After a few months spent walking in Wales, very often sleeping in the open air, feeding on what nature had to offer, or on the hospitality of local villagers in exchange for the few services he could render, he arrived in London, where he found shelter in a deserted house in Greek Street, Soho. The days and most of the nights were spent 'sitting in the parks or elsewhere' or prowling ceaselessly down the streets of London. The prostitutes and the watchmen were his friends.

Ann, a sixteen-year-old wretch, whose goodness of heart had survived her degradation, once spent her last coin to buy him a stimulant when exhaustion had made him faint. One day when they were to meet, she was not there; he spent months studying all the links that might take him to her, he searched in anguish and with desperation, he saw her at every corner of every street, but she could never be found. Throughout his life he was haunted by visions of Ann and dreams of finding and losing her, never sure if they were really dreams.

Visions and hallucinations played a fundamental role in his life well before he fell prey to the ravages of opium. Possibly because of the impact of his sister's death, or because of an arrested development in his own emotional make up which allowed him to retain the simplicity of a child, his relationships with children were the strongest emotions he ever felt which were not connected with himself and his self-torture. With Kate Wordsworth, the poet's young child, he established profound contact. 'I had always viewed her as an impersonation of the dawn and the spirit of infancy', he wrote in *Confessions of an English Opium-eater*. When she died he was to spend many nights by her grave where, he wrote, 'I saw her at the opposite side of the field which might sometimes be at a distance of $\frac{1}{4}$ of a mile, generally not so much'.

The nature of his dreams was altered by the development of his drug addiction. While at Oxford, after his London days of vagrancy, he was recommended opium by a friend for neuralgic pains. 'Here was a panacea for all human woes: here was the secret of happiness about which philosophers had disputed for so many ages, at once discovered: happiness might now be bought for a penny, and carried in the waistcoat pocket.' For eight years, until 1812, happiness was his. While he read widely, from metaphysics to economics, and wrote literary criticisms for journals and magazines, at least once a week when evening fell, there would be the opium decanter with red-brown laudanum by his side. He became an apologist for opium, an expert in its effects, using it not only for its negative results in the mere relief of pain, but as an intellectual stimulant and exhilarant. By 1813 he had changed from being an intermittent opium-taker to a confirmed opium-eater, and he entered a period of terror and strife.

He was invaded by a sense of sinking, as if into unmeasured depths. Darkness became painted with ceaseless processions of awful pictures in which the dreams and agonies of youth were mixed to inextricable confusion with stories woven from classical or oriental reminiscence: 'I grew afraid to sleep; and I shrunk from it as from the most savage tortures.' 'I sometimes seemed to have lived for 70 or 100 years in one night; nay, sometimes had feelings representative of a millennium passed in that time.' His dreams began as splendid architectural visions of cities and palaces, became lakes and silvery expanses of water, seas and oceans, to sink into scenes of deepening oriental extravagance and physical horrors of ugly

Wordsworth's Cottage, *near Patterdale in the Lake District, where De Quincey resided for a time with Words-worth and Coleridge.*

birds, snakes, and crocodiles.

In 1816, at the age of thirty-one, he married Margaret Simpson, who was eighteen, and this and the urgency of his work helped him to reduce his daily allowance from eight thousand drops of laudanum to a thousand drops. 'The cloud of profoundest melancholy' which had rested on his brain lifted, only to descend again with more vigour and cruelty. Then began the desperate battle to free himself from a paradise which had become hell, so poignantly described in the *Confessions*. But every victory was met by a relapse, whether he tried reducing the dose or the torture of total abstinence. Only in 1848 did his wrestlings seem to have come to an end with the find of the minimum dose which made existence endurable, and to it he had to keep for the rest of his life.

In the same way that opium had brought to light the faculty of daydreaming, of projecting visual images or fancies from De Quincey's mind into the air, which he had constitutionally enjoyed since he was a child, so too opium intensified aspects of his personality which might have remained latent, or at least subdued, without the drug. His inability to cope with reality translated itself into every aspect of practical life. Predictably, he was astoundingly incompetent in all financial matters. While still a young man, kept on a strict allowance by his guardian, he became involved in borrowing money at exorbitant rates of interest from a firm of London jews; later, most of his capital was lost in the failures of great business enterprises. His precarious financial status at no point taught him prudence or tempered his extravagance.

His readiness to befriend others led him to part with large sums of money, including three hundred pounds to Coleridge, or to make loans that were never repaid. He lived on the boundless expectations of what he might earn from writing, often failing to satisfy these expectations from either illness or a distaste for commercial writing. He despised and dismissed all that was gross or material. 'Those who knew him a little', wrote Burton, 'might call him a loose man in money-matters; those who knew him closer, laughed at the idea of coupling any notion of pecuniary or other like responsibilities with his nature. Only immediate craving necessities could ever extract from him an acknowledgement of the common vulgar agencies by which men subsist in civilized society, and only while the necessity lasted did the acknowledgement exist.' Thus he was constantly in financial trouble and this accounted for much of his eccentric conduct.

While living in Edinburgh he was considered different from any other mortal because his whereabouts could never be known; he would never reveal his place of abode because he felt constantly persecuted by creditors. His difficulties did not only arise from a fundamental lack of money, but also from a total inability to have the right amount at the right time, or to take the practical steps to secure it. One night he arrived at the house of a friend begging to be provided with seven shillings and sixpence. Seeing his friend's surprise he said he had a 'document' that could serve as guarantee, and rummaging in his pockets and fetching a miscellany of small articles out of them, he produced a crumpled piece of paper: it was a fifty pound note. His friend tells us that his impression was that, had he accepted it in exchange, he probably would never have heard about it again.

His elusiveness meant that his presence at social occasions could never be relied on; when invited he would invariably accept but very rarely turn up. If his presence was really required he had to be found and brought. On one particular occasion when a messenger was sent to collect him for a dinner, he followed meekly and his arrival is described by someone present:

> He opens the door and fetches in the little stranger. What can it be? A street-boy of some sort? His costume, in fact, is a boy's duffle great-coat, very threadbare, with a hole in it, and buttoned tight to the chin, where it meets the fragments of

Portrait of De Quincey *as a young man, perhaps at the time of his marriage to Margaret Simpson in 1816. It was after her death that his habits and appearance became notably bizarre, his dwellings invaded by beggars and submerged under piles of papers so that he was periodically forced to lock the door on them and move elsewhere.*

a parti-coloured belcher hankerchief; on his feet are list-shoes, covered with snow, for it is a stormy winter night. What can be the theory of such a costume? The simplest thing in the world – it consisted of the fragments of apparel nearest at hand. Had chance thrown to him a court single-breasted coat, with a bishop's apron, a kilt, and top-boots, in these he would have made his entry.

Once his company had been obtained it was often very difficult to get rid of him. He was an excellent conversationalist, taking his listeners to his own dream-land, telling of visions that had come upon him in his walks among the mountains.

The recollections of his daughter confirm this picture of his inadequacy when faced by the practicalities of life. He did not care, nor would he let others care, for his dress. 'Those not accustomed to eccentric habits got the impression of poverty', we are told, but the truth was that if a thought occurred to him while dressing or undressing, 'he would stop with his coat just taken off or not put on, without stockings at all, or with one off and one on, and becoming lost in what grew out of this thought, he would work on for hours'. If visitors were to arrive, rather than keep them waiting, he would receive them in whatever state of dress he was in. A visitor in 1853 described him as the 'strangest mixture of an appear-ance so neglected that he looks like an old beggar, of manners so perfect that they would do honour to a prince, and of conversation unapproached for brilliancy'.

He was a creature of the night. He sat and wrote then, refreshing himself with tea or coffee in large quantities, and went to bed in the early hours to wake at midday. Often his 'thin light figure' could be seen wandering in the country lanes on starlit rambles. His habits were simple and almost ascetic. Early on he lost his teeth as a result of the excesses of opium, so he lived on soup, coffee, bread and a little wine. His belief that 'misery is the talisman by which man communicates with the world outside of our fleshly world' made him vulnerable to the suffering of others. His daughter wrote after his death that when he was at home, a crowd of beggars would invade 'among whom borrowed babies and drunken old women were sure of the largest sympathy; but he refused it to none, and he was often wearied by the necessity he laid upon himself of listening to all the woes which were heaped upon him'.

After his wife died, it was the efforts of his daughters which enabled some semblance of domestic order to survive. He set a morbid value on his papers and would not allow them to be disturbed. He scattered them all over his room until there was not a square inch of space on the table, no possibility of making his bed, for the weight of papers gathered there, no chair to sit on and no floor to walk on to get from the door to the fireplace. Living in lodgings in Edinburgh or London, when his room had become 'snowed up', he would simply lock the door and move

THE incidents recorded in the Preliminary Confessions, lie within a period of which the earlier extreme is now rather more, and the latter extreme less, than nineteen years ago: consequently, in a popular way of computing dates, many of the incidents might be indifferently referred to a distance of eighteen or of nineteen years; and, as the notes and memoranda for this narrative were drawn up originally about last Christmas, it seemed most natural in all cases to prefer the former date. In the hurry of composing the narrative, though some months had then elapsed, this date was every where retained: and, in many cases,

Foreword of 'Confessions of an English Opium-eater', *an account of his addiction, from the first edition of 1822.*

somewhere else. When he died there were six places where he had these deposits. There were rumours at the time that 'in his den there were seen a sort of rubble-work inner-wall of volumes with their edges outwards, while others, bound and unbound – the plebeian sheepskin and the aristocratic Russian – were squeezed into certain tubs drawn from the washing establishment of a confiding landlady'.

When his room caught fire, he would not allow the use of water because his papers might get wet. It was only on rare nights that he did not set something on fire: one of his children would look up from their work or book to say casually, 'Papa your hair is on fire'; 'Is it my love?' and a hand would rub out the blaze. But on occasions the placidity was broken and he would be precipitated violently into whirlwinds of impatience 'that would seem insanities, but are not such in fact', as he wrote 'my understanding is never under any delusion'.

> Whatever I may have been writing is suddenly wrapt, as it were, in one sheet of consuming fire – the very paper is poisoned to my eyes. I cannot endure to look at it and I sweep it away into vast piles of unfinished letters or inchoate essays begun and interrupted under circumstances the same in kind, though differing unaccountably in degree.

The impression he left among his contemporaries was that he escaped all the conventional patterns of logic. To explain him was an attempt to describe the indescribable: 'were we to attempt to tell all about him, no man could believe it, so separate would the whole be from all the normal conditions of human nature.'

Ouida

Life should be a perpetual Kyrie Eleison: instead of which it is only a chorus of Offenbach's.   STRATHMORE

Max Beerbohm dedicated his collection of essays, *More*, to 'Mlle de la Ramée with the author's compliments, and to Ouida with his love'. It was a happy thought, and a subtle, even poignant, comment on its subject, for Ouida's own life was curiously at variance with the lurid *bizarrerie* of the characters she created, and the air of mystery tinged with impropriety which surrounded her name.

Ouida's particular talents and eccentricities exactly fitted the style and pace of late Victorian England; she wrote highly successful society novels, condemning the movement for women's emancipation on the grounds that it was a deliberate unarming of her sex, a denial of a woman's proper skills. She opposed vivisection. She wrote against armaments, decried the growing power of the State, and complained bitterly at the vulgarity and coarseness of modern life. 'Art', she wrote, 'is rather an intellectual dissipation than a tenderness of sentiment', and taste in England 'is now only a tradition smothered under cigar ash and buried in a gun case.'

At the height of her fame, in the 1880s and early '90s, she contributed articles to all the major literary reviews, and her novels and short stories were acclaimed by an increasing public. 'Her every page', wrote Max Beerbohm, 'is a riot of unpolished epigrams and unpolished poetry of vision, with a hundred discursions and redundancies.' By the time of her death in 1908 she had long outlived her vogue, and *The Times* obituary noted sadly that she died 'leaving, it is to be feared, no such imperishable name in English literature as she fondly imagined'. In her last years the memory of her great successes sustained her amidst isolation, ridicule and growing eccentricity.

Ouida was born Marie Louise de la Ramée on New Year's Day, 1839, in Bury St Edmunds. Her inability to pronounce her own name easily led her cousins to rechristen her 'Ouida', which was the nearest she could come to 'Louise'. Her

Marie Louise de la Ramée (1839–1908), *known as Ouida, drawn by Alice Danyell in 1878. She was called Ouida by her cousins when a child and later she used it as a* nom de plume.

parents were an oddly assorted couple. Her father, Louis Ramée, was a Frenchman about whom almost nothing is known, save that he arrived in Bury St Edmunds sometime in the late 1830s, set up as a teacher of his native language and played havoc with the hearts of the young ladies of the town. Ramée claimed that he came as an emissary of Louis Napoleon Bonaparte, the future Napoleon III, but his listeners were generally puzzled as to what the Bonapartist pretender hoped for from the good burgesses of Bury. This reflection, however, generally came to them in the privacy of their own homes, for Monsieur Ramée was gifted with enormous charm and an inimitable gift for phrase, as well as the armour of mystery. In 1838 he married Susan Sutton, the youngest and prettiest of three daughters of a local family of modest but tangible wealth.

Ouida was the only child of this unlikely union and came early to find sympathy and excitement in the company of her father rather than her mother. She went with him to Boulogne, to the Great Exhibition of 1851, and saw with him the funeral of the Duke of Wellington in the following year. Her delight in her father's company was intensified by his prolonged absences from home which he put down to his growing importance and involvement with the Bonapartist cause. He used to fill his impressionable daughter's head with wild tales of daring escapes and secret rendezvous, of foul deeds in lonely castles and the bright chivalry that lit up this dangerous and dedicated life. Small wonder that Ouida spent a large part of her rather self-absorbed and lonely childhood contemplating the colourful and dramatic world which lay beyond the confines of Suffolk.

From her mother, Ouida learned an appreciation of the countryside and its wildlife. This delight in animals became in time the foundation for one of her most abiding eccentricities, her passion for dogs. She looked upon dogs as creatures gifted with as great a capacity for suffering as their masters, and an infinitely greater fund of loyalty and compassion. She believed that truly great men were invariably dog lovers: 'I think it is the frank, free, fond faith of the creature which is so welcome a contrast to them with the world of flatterers and of foes'. This sympathy she extended to all living creatures, involving herself in the Anti-Vivisection Movement and taking up the work of the Guild of Gentleness, a society formed in Manchester to protect small animals, birds and insects from the hazards of 'modern improvement'.

In 1857 Ouida and her mother came to London, to a house in Ravenscourt Park. It appears that Louis Ramée's frequent absences, and the strange manners of his unapproachable daughter, made a retirement from Suffolk if not imperative, at least tactful. One result of the move to London was that Ouida confided her literary ambitions to their new Doctor, Francis Ainsworth, who introduced her

Dust cover of an edition of 'Held in Bondage', *first published in 1863. This was the first time the name Ouida was attached to her writing. 'Regaining consciousness' after reading her work, Max Beerbohm described her as 'that unique, flamboyant lady, one of the miracles of modern literature'.*

to his cousin, the novelist and editor W. Harrison Ainsworth. The literary Ainsworth was at once struck by Ouida's obvious sincerity and delighted by some of her compositions, which already included a history of England written at the age of fourteen. Ouida's first published story was entitled 'Dashwood's Drag' and appeared in *Bentley's Miscellany* in April 1859.

Ouida's celebrity as a writer of short stories, most of them set in wonderfully romantic settings, of which she had no direct knowledge, led her on to write longer novels in part form. *The New Monthly Magazine* published 'Granville de Vigne' as a serial in 1863, and one month after its last appearance in that form the ever enterprising Tinsley brothers published it as a complete novel under the title *Held in Bondage*. Thereafter Ouida never looked back; her success was such, and the demand for her books so great, that within five years she wrote as many major novels, including her best, *Strathmore*, and the most popular, *Under Two Flags*. The final accolade came in 1866, when Baron Tauchnitz offered to include several of her novels in his famous series, in which the best contemporary British authors were introduced to a Continental readership. Tauchnitz and Ouida became firm friends, and the Tauchnitz family helped Ouida through good fortune and ill until the year of her death. From the early 1880s she was often desperate for money, living as she did in a grand style, and Tauchnitz regularly had to help her out of situations made awful by her own wilfulness and intransigence.

By 1867 Ouida had made so much money from her novels, both in book form and on the stage, that she moved, with her mother, to Welbeck Street. Her earnings reached over £5,000 a year, and the stay in Welbeck Street was a brief one: towards the end of 1867 she and her mother and accompanying dogs moved into the Langham Hotel (now part of the BBC). From this time onwards Ouida, never looked upon as a conventional figure, became more and more eccentric and outrageous. She was so excessively conscious of her own plain, ungarnished appearance that she henceforth declined to ask women to her already famous parties, making a sole exception of the wife of Sir Richard Burton. The novelist, accompanied always by the retiring figure of her mother, entertained huge concourses of men, mostly military men, adventurers or people of unconventional background or occupation. Guardsmen were her especial delight: 'now gentlemen,' she used to say, 'smoke and drink as if you were at the club; talk as if you were in the smoking room there and never think about us'.

Ouida's extraordinary absorption in herself and her writing made her quite insensitive to other people's feelings; she acquired a reputation for rudeness and tactlessness belied utterly by her restrained, un-Bohemian manner, and such was the oddly frantic interest in the bizarre in social life, she was eagerly sought after

Illustration from 'Punch', *1878, entitled 'Strapmore. A Romance by Weeder Author of Folly and Farin, Under Two Rags, Arryadn'ty, Chuck, Two Little Wooden Jews, Nicotine, A horse with Glanders, In Somers Town, Shamdross, etc.', a parody of Ouida's novel 'Strathmore'.*

as a dinner guest in consequence. 'A little scandal', she used to say, 'is an excellent thing.'

One of her favourites at the Langham was the Confederate General Breckinridge, and she lost no time in allowing rumours of a liaison to escape. In fact, it is highly unlikely that they were anything more than friends, but Ouida was not content with the suggestion; she started on a course which she pursued all her life, of fabricating romances for herself on a grand scale in a manner which rapidly became demonstrative and public, and acutely embarrassing to the objects of her strange love. There was one even more bizarre twist: before long she began to believe that it was not she who was in love but the other. For the last forty years of her life she went through a series of well-publicized romances with people who in most cases had barely exchanged civilities with her. Her first such entanglement came in 1870 with the great Italian tenor, Mario. Ouida made an astonishing scene at Covent Garden in July 1871, when she flung a bouquet into the arms of the singer, out of which dropped an ivory cigarette case and note made up of quotations from Dante so unmistakable in meaning as to cause the Italian to stand in bewilderment. Surprise turned to wrath, and Mario lost no time in rebuffing the incautious overtures of the infatuated Ouida.

93

Ouida *at the time when she was eagerly sought after as a dinner guest because of her bizarre and outrageous manner.*

In the autumn of 1871 Ouida and her mother went to Brussels, the setting for *A Dog of Flanders*, the most poignant and readable of Ouida's dog stories. The pair went on to Florence; 'where lies the secret spell of Florence?' wrote Ouida, 'a spell that strengthens, and does not fade with time'. Ouida lived in Florence for the next twenty-three years, never once returning to London; she turned her back on England, on all the sights and sounds which had nourished and amused her for so long. It seems that the fame of the Langham period, with its accompanying notoriety had unsettled her and made her restless for the world which she described with such felicity in her novels; also, she was beginning to be bored with the prospect of turning into just one more literary institution. Florence, 'the beautiful small city set among its shining waters, with all the grace of classic descent, its repose of contemplative rest, its sanctity of imperishable greatness', became her home and the scene of her gradual transformation from one of the city's compulsive attractions to one of its saddest embarrassments.

Florence, at that time, had a spirit and *élan* without rival in Europe; the winter season there was especially brilliant, and Ouida threw herself into the endless round of parties and receptions with renewed vigour. Early in her stay she met the Marchese Lotteringhi Della Stufa, a gentleman-in-waiting to the King of Italy and thenceforth the acknowledged passion of Ouida's life. She determined to take up residence in Florence and took the Villa Farinola at Scandicci in 1874, where she lived for fifteen years.

During that time she wrote with undiminished vigour, devoting herself to an evocation of the Italian landscape and people unique among British writers of the time. The Villa Rocaldi in *Friendship* is a perfect description of her own home, and *Pascarel* is a brilliant portrait of Florence in the 1870s. Ouida became increasingly odd as the years passed; she developed an extraordinary love of white things, and her ponies, her carriages, even her clothes, were all made or bought in that colour. She gave grand receptions, clad in white satin if the theme of her current book was socially elevated, or white muslin if the story had to do with humbler folk. Gradually, the expense of such a household with its large gardens and staff told on her now dwindling finances. From the early 1880s onwards she became enmeshed in financial crises, lawsuits and endless wranglings with her various publishers.

In 1894 she was compelled to leave the Villa Farinola and retire to Lucca, a town she came to loathe. Growing poverty, a declining reputation and the death of many of her established friends left her isolated in a way undreamt of during the triumphant period in Florence. Her eccentricities stood out in sinister contrast to her reduced surroundings. She clung pathetically to her dogs, of whom there were sometimes as many as forty, becoming more self-centred and unapproachable as the years went by. Her mother died in 1896 and the last eight or ten years of her life were spent in virtual isolation. Ouida died from the effects of pneumonia on 25 January, 1908; her death evoked a wave of public interest and sympathy, and the story of the novelist's last pathetic years was somehow transformed into a saga of poverty and courage worthy of one of her own novels.

In *Views and Opinions*, published in 1895, Ouida set out her concept of the novelist's role:

> The supreme gift of the true artist is a rapidity of perception and comprehension which is totally unlike the slow piecemeal observations of others. As the musician reads the pages of a score at a glance, as the author comprehends the essence of a book by a flash of intelligence, as the painter sees at a glance the points and lines and hues of a landscape, whilst the ordinary man plods through the musical compositions note by note, the book page by page, the landscape detail by detail, so the true artist, whether poet, painter or dramatist sees human nature, penetrating its disguises and embracing all its force and weakness by that insight which is within him.
>
> When the true poet or artist takes up in his hand a single garden pear or russet apple, he will behold, through its suggestions, as in a sorcerer's mirror, a whole smiling land of orchard and of meadow; he will smell the sweet scent of ripe fruit and wet leaves; he will tread a thousand grassy ways and wade in a thousand rippling streams; he will hear the matins bell and the evensong, the lowing kine, and the bleating flocks; he will think in a second of time of the trees which were in blossom when Drake and Raleigh sailed, and the fields which were green when Tudor and Valois met, and the sunsets of long, long ago when Picardy was in the flames of war and all over the Norman lands the bowmen tramped and the fair Knights rode.

The passage is worth quoting at length because it is a perfect illustration of Ouida's own method of writing; the prose gathers pace as that over bright imagination conjures up images at once brilliantly colourful, suggestive and unfinished; the speed of her pen is such that the reader has a sense of being swirled past the jutting and awkward details and given over entirely to dizzying effects of sensation and excitement. As Max Beerbohm wrote: 'her pen gathers new strength of its every dip into the ink-pot.' This method of writing and the sustained vitality of her output troubled and occasionally exasperated Ouida's critics. The exaggeration of her style, the absurdity of many of her characters, and the frequent inaccuracy of her descriptions, made her a perfect butt for those critics who preferred consciously artistic writers, reticent, economical and with a stricter eye for truth. But those who were prepared to put themselves under her spell, to enter that artificial but convincing world, found rich rewards. Beerbohm described himself as 'regaining consciousness' after being stunned and over-powered by the writing of 'that unique, flamboyant lady, one of the miracles of modern literature'. Wilfrid Scawen Blunt, a sterner critic, thought Ouida's novels 'to be the only English novels which can at all be compared with Balzac's as giving a vivid and life-like picture of the larger world of society, women as well as men, they describe'.

Ouida, in common with many novelists, wrote and re-wrote her own obituary as a writer. Her truest attempt was in a letter to *The Times* in October 1883, an odd vehicle and an early date for such a composition. 'To many of us', she wrote, 'the world seems a marvellous union of tragedy and comedy, which run side by side like twin children; like a web of Tyrian looms with the gold threads crossing and recrossing on the dark purple of its intricate meshes . . . I do not object to realism in fiction; what I object to is the limitation of realism in fiction to what is commonplace, tedious and bald – is the habit, in a word, of insisting that the potato is real and that the passion flower is not'.

Punch's Fancy Portraits No 45, *1881. 'O fie! 'tis an unweeded garden'.* Hamlet, *Act I, Scene 2, a caricature of Ouida.*

Squire Waterton

Our pleasure in ourselves would suffer sadly if Charles Waterton were not called eccentric, for few of us are so full of life, love, curiosity and plain joy that we dare consider him normal. He has been called a saint, he rode a crocodile, travelled far, bounded high; he shames us. A comfortable cotton wool laps most of our small mistakes, and it is disconcerting to read of a man who had so little cotton wool about him that he remembered for nearly forty years that he had 'once treated a family of Badgers very ill' when he turned them out of his park to make it safe for birds. The park was Walton Hall, an estate in Yorkshire with a lake, woods and pastures, and here Charles' interest in natural history began when he was a child.

After school at Stoneyhurst, Charles spent a year at home and then began his travels with a visit to Spain, but yellow fever, or 'the black vomit', drove him home to Walton. Later, his father and uncle sent him to Demerara to look after the family estates. While he was there, they died, and at the age of twenty-three Charles inherited his father's new house and Walton Hall; he certainly had every advantage and he used it to the full. From Demerara he started his travels.

Charles Waterton's publications include his autobiography, three books of essays on natural history, and several long contentious letters to other naturalists, but his masterpiece is *Wanderings in South America*, which was published in 1825. Open it at the preface and the heart sinks: 'I offer this book of "Wanderings" with a hesitating hand. It has little merit, and must make its way through the world as well as it can'. We have read such words, usually written with reason, too many times. Turn to page one:

First Journey . . . In the month of April 1812 I left the town of Starbroek to travel through the wilds of Demerara and Esquibo . . . The chief objects in view were to collect a quantity of the strongest wourali poison and to reach the inland frontier-fort . . . The road for horses . . . extends a very little way, and even ends before the cultivation of the plantations ceases . . . Higher up stand the sugar-works of Amelia's Waard, solitary and abandoned; and after passing these there is not a ruin to inform the traveller that either coffee or sugar have ever been cultivated.

Charles Waterton, Esq. *from 'The Illustrated London News' of 24 August, 1844. Describing himself, Waterton wrote: 'I stand six feet high, all but half an inch. On looking at myself in the glass, I can see at once that my face is anything but comely: continued exposure to the sun, and to the rains of the tropics, has furrowed it in places, and given it a tint which neither Rowland's Kalydor nor all the cosmetics on Belinda's toilette, would ever be able to remove'.*

Walton Hall on Waterton's estate in Yorkshire, where he built a high wall round the park and founded the first bird sanctuary. His lakeside tomb is shown in this engraving.

One man may write 'I opened the door and walked out', and we shut the book; another may write the same words and we go outside with him; if he collects birds, so do we.

By 1812 almost every bird, beast, insect and flower that had been discovered had also been classified and nailed firmly to the dissecting board by a Latin name understood by naturalists everywhere. The logic of this is beyond question and has long been accepted; Confucius held that civilization began with the naming of things, and Adam's first recorded act in Eden was to name the animals – and what is the use of such labour if we cannot all understand it if we want to? Against logic, though, we must set: 'Give a dog a bad name and hang him': the name once given colours further thought and observation.

Charles would use no Latin names; he used the simplest ones, and these he queried too. He wrote up his notes . . . 'I intended to have written much more at length; but days and months and years have passed away, and nothing has been done . . . Thinking that I shall never have patience enough to sit down and write a full account of all I saw and examined in those remote wilds, I give up . . . and

Portrait of Charles Waterton (1782–1865) *by Percy Fitzgerald, 1860. He is portrayed with two examples of taxidermy, which was his principal interest and the reason for much of his astonishing bravery as a traveller.*

send forth this account . . . just as it was written at the time'. So, instead of care-fully reasoned conclusions, we read of his new delight in each bird and animal he saw, and we follow his changes of opinion between his four journeys. The free style of the writing and the imprecise names made other naturalists ('closet naturalists', he called them) unwilling to accept his discoveries, but the study of natural history was certainly changed by his increasing refusal to accept the old word, his own or anyone else's, and more naturalists took to field work.

The sloth was his most famous doubted word. In 1812, he saw what all the other naturalists saw:

> His looks, his gestures and his cries all conspire to entreat you to take pity on him. These are the only weapons of defence which Nature hath given him . . . he cannot escape from you . . . It is said his piteous moans make the tiger relent and turn out of the way . . . Do not then level your gun at him or pierce him with a poisoned arrow – he has never hurt one living creature. A few leaves, and those of the commonest and coarsest kind, are all he asks for his support . . . He has no soles to his feet nor has he the power of moving his toes separately. His hair is flat, and puts you in mind of grass withered by the wintry blast. His legs are too short; they appear deformed . . . and his claws are disproportionably long. Were you to mark down, upon a graduated scale, the different claims to superiority amongst the four-footed animals, this poor ill-formed creature's claim would be the last upon the lowest degree.

By 1820, Charles had had time to look at the sloth more carefully and to keep one for several months:

> Those who have written on this singular animal have remarked that he is in a perpetual state of pain . . . proverbially slow . . . a prisoner in space, and that, as soon as he has consumed all the leaves of the tree upon which he had mounted, he rolls himself up in the form of a ball and then falls to the ground. This is not the case. If the naturalists who have written the history of the sloth had gone into the wilds in order to examine his haunts and economy, they would not have drawn the foregoing conclusions. They would have learned that, though all other quadrupeds may be described while resting on the ground, the sloth is an exception to this rule, and that his history must be written while he is in the tree. [This is then most thoroughly done] . . . it is but fair to surmise that it just enjoys life as much as any other animal.

The fourth journey began in North America in 1824 when Charles 'landed in health and merriment in the stately capital of the New World'. Near Buffalo, he sprained his ankle, and remembered that his doctor in England had prescribed the pump for a previous sprain. What better than the greater power of Niagara? But, 'I was obliged to drop it'. After another visit to Demerara he returned to England and thenceforth stayed mostly at home.

One of the first things he did there, in 1826, was to begin building a high wall all round the park and declare that no guns might be brought in, nothing shot; Walton Hall became the first bird sanctuary and Charles the first birdwatcher to build a hide. This was when he moved out the badgers and foxes, as predators of

ABOVE: Mr Waterton mounted on the cayman, when living, *illustrating one of his remarkable adventures in South America. He wrote, not surprisingly, that it was the first and last time he ever rode a crocodile.*

BELOW: Experiments with rattlesnakes at Leeds. *Waterton obtained some Wourali poison from the Macoushi Indians in 1812 and he is shown here gauging its efficacy as compared with that of the poison of the rattlesnake.*

Sketch of Charles Waterton *by Percy Fitzgerald.*

the eggs and chicks of ground-nesting birds, though the equally guilty (and more mobile) crows and ravens were birds, and therefore safe.

Some of Charles Waterton's neighbours disapproved of this, and undoubtedly of his whole way of life; while others grew stout and gouty, the healthy, thin and offensively anti-alcohol Charles bounced with undiminished energy, on and on and on. It was not enough for him to climb to the top of a large oak at the age of eighty; he was surprised and hurt that no one else wanted to go up with him. His friend Dr Richard Hobson wrote that he had frequently seen the Squire 'when beyond seventy years of age, hop on one leg along the brink of a rock forming the highest terrace in the grotto, whilst the other leg was dangling over the chasm below . . . he would return again by hopping back on the contrary leg'. At first one wonders if jealousy did not make Charles refuse to let Blondin perform on a tight-rope over the lake – but surely the act would have been boring to the man who had stood on one foot on top of the head of the angel on top of the Castello di Sant'Angelo?

He returned from one trip to Rome with cages full of owls, which he kindly but most fatally bathed; he tried in vain to get a Vampire bat to suck blood from his big toe; he made wings to fly with (Dr Hobson gives no details of the mechanism but he was persuaded not to start too high); and if there was nothing else to do he made something up, a Night-Mare, or a sheep with a horn growing out of its ear.

His masterwork of inventive taxidermy was the Nondescript, made as a knock-out demonstration of his new techniques. Inspiration came on the fourth journey when he skinned a Red Howler monkey for the pot and observed it to be:

> So like a young one of our own species that a delicate stomach might possibly revolt at the idea of putting a knife and fork into it . . . However . . . not to be sneezed at when boiled in cayenne pepper or roasted on a stick over a good fire.

I mentioned in a former adventure, that I had hit upon an entirely new plan of making the skins of quadrupeds retain their exact form and feature. Intense application to the subject has enabled me to . . . hit the character of an animal to a very great nicety, even to the preservation of the pouting lip, dimples, warts and wrinkles on the face . . . I also procured an animal which has caused not a little speculation and astonishment . . . his face and head cause the inspector to pause . . . The features of the animal are quite of the Grecian cast . . . Some gentlemen of great skill and talent . . . were convinced that the whole series of its features had been changed. Others again have hesitated . . . not being able to make up their minds whether it be possible that the brute features of the monkey can be changed into the noble countenance of man.

It was another Red Howler, worked over. It did not endear Charles to the closet naturalists.

His new method was to soak the skin in a solution of corrosive sublimate in ammonia, which both preserved the skin and kept it free of insects. Then it was gently dried and gradually worked from inside with 'a little stick the size of a common knitting-needle' into the shape of life. Birds were stuffed with cotton, but larger specimens were hollow, without stuffing or armature of any kind. Some still survive, but modern taxidermists are not interested in even trying the technique.

The Nondescript, *Waterton's masterwork of inventive taxidermy, a Red Howler monkey worked over.*

Charles had strong ideas about many other things: politics, one special customs officer called Lushington, the horrors of tight-lacing and strangling cravats, pillows, soft beds, too many clothes and too much hair: himself, he had a crew cut. Indeed there are so many things to tell that his biographers have trouble choosing; Dr Hobson was perpetually surprised by Charles' health (and so are we, for he bled himself constantly); Father Wood, himself a naturalist, concentrated on the natural history; Edith Sitwell tells us of the long heritage of saintliness, with Sir Thomas More and six other saints in his ancestry; Richard Aldington is sarcastic. Philip Gosse's is the most balanced account, but it is the *Wanderings* that cast the spell. We have only space for a few stages in the collection of the wourali poison and for the crocodile. Wourali is the chief ingredient of curare – Macbeth's witches would have loved it:

> A day or two before the Macoushi Indian prepares the poison he goes into the forest in quest of the ingredients. A vine grows in these wilds which is called wourali . . . When he has procured enough of this he digs up a root of a very bitter taste, ties them together, and then looks about for two kinds of bulbous plants which contain a green and glutinous juice. He fills a little quake which he carries on his back with the stalks of these; and lastly ranges up and down till he finds two species of ants. One of them is very large and black, and so venomous that its sting produces a fever . . . The other is a little red ant . . . After obtaining these he has no more need to range the forest.
>
> A quantity of the strongest Indian pepper is used, but this he has already planted round his hut. The pounded fangs of the labarri snake and those of the counacouchi are likewise added . . . he scrapes the wourali vine and bitter root into thin shavings and puts them into a kind of colander made of leaves . . . pours water on the shavings . . . the liquor which comes through has the appearance of coffee . . . Lastly, the snakes' fangs, ants and pepper are bruised and thrown into it . . . placed on a slow fire . . . till reduced to a thick syrup of a deep brown colour.

The crocodile, or cayman, was hard to get, but at last one was caught with baited hooks on a rope. The Indians wanted to kill it at once, but Charles wanted the skin undamaged. He armed himself with a mast and the men pulled the cayman out of the river: 'I saw he was in a state of fear and perturbation. I instantly dropped the mast, sprung up and jumped on his back . . . I immediately seized his forelegs, and my main force twisted them on his back; thus they served me for a bridle . . . he began to plunge furiously, and lashed the sand with his long and powerful tail . . . it was the first and last time I was ever on a cayman's back.'

So he got his skin, ten and a half feet long, and for once he was cruel.

The cigar-box colours of the jungle and the flashing birds were left behind in 1824, and the colours of his second forty years must be seen as the English grass

Charles Waterton's funeral: the procession of boats on the lake, *from 'The Illustrated London News' of 17 June, 1865. It is said that the birds from the sanctuary in the park at Walton Hall followed his funeral boat in a long flight across the water.*

and stone grey of Yorkshire, but never as dull. The house was on an island in the lake, and was a museum of his collections and contrivances. Across an iron foot-bridge was his new green paradise with a semi-circle of yews, a ruin and a grotto. Picnickers were encouraged, cups and saucers provided, mill workers invited for the day, local lunatics to dinner. Fires were kept up in the grotto all through the year, not only for Charles, who felt the cold, but for his beloved cats, and for their benefit no one might smoke there.

Charles Waterton died in 1865 and was buried by the lake. A contemporary print shows the procession of dark boats, and there are accounts of local mourning. Accounts, too, of the birds gathering from the woods and fields of their sanctuary and following his funeral boat in a long flight across the water.

Jack Mytton

John Mytton was born on 30 September, 1796, and before he was two years old was left fatherless – an example of the curious disposition in Mytton's family to occupy an early grave: neither his grandfather nor his great-grandfather lived to see their sons come of age, and Mytton himself lived to be only thirty-eight. The Squire's recklessness may perhaps be attributed in part to this early loss, for his widowed mother tended to dote in no small measure upon her weird offspring, of whom she lost control at an early stage.

His career at Westminster School was terminated abruptly after a year, in which time he spent £800, double his allowance. He lasted four days at Harrow; no one knows why. Conducted to a private tutor in Berkshire, he suddenly broke this good man's head, thus sullying their relationship forever. Pressure from the chaplain of Halston, something of a rip himself, forced Mytton to enter himself at Oxford, but only on the condition that he be expected to read nothing besides the *Racing Calendar* and the *Stud Book*. The last visible evidence of his interest in higher education was his order for three pipes of port wine to be sent addressed to him at Cambridge.

At the age of nineteen, after a year's tour of the Continent, he joined the Seventh Hussars and served with them in France as part of the army of occupation. He appears to have been deeply hurt that there was no more fighting to be had there, so he confined himself to racing and the systematic losing of great sums of money at gambling tables, one of which, following a £3,000 loss, he smashed to atoms by way of compensation.

Shortly after coming into his enormous fortune, which included his ancestral home of Halston, near Shrewsbury, as well as extensive lands in North Wales, he bade farewell to the military profession and in 1818 took to matrimony, allying himself with Harriet Emma Jones, daughter of Sir Tyrwhitt Jones, of Stanley Hall, Shropshire. This wife, who was very delicate, died within a few years leaving only one daughter. Mytton, after a very decent interval, remarried, but this second partner, one Caroline Giffard, deserted her Squire because she could not take much more of him and his awful ways.

Left, we are told, to his own devices, Mytton proceeded to extract from life the

The 'Meet', with Lord Derby's Stag hounds, *a print by the famous sporting artist, Henry Alken, published by Rudolph Ackermann. Alken was commissioned to illustrate the first full-length biography of Jack Mytton by 'Nimrod', Charles James Apperley, a Shropshire contemporary and friend of Mytton. The incident shown here is Mytton's visit by coach to look at the Stag hounds when, because of his dandified appearance, he was mistaken for a London tailor.*

fullest measure of enjoyment, according to his own peculiar lights. Here began the fun; and his incredible escapades soon became notorious, while his extraordinary powers of endurance and utter fearlessness, allied to astonishing physical and constitutional strength, afforded his neighbours a never-ending source of wonderment.

Everyone, it seems, who has been moved to write of John Mytton, has found it necessary to adopt in some measure an apologetic tone. 'Nimrod', Charles James Apperley, a Shropshire contemporary and friend of Mytton, has coloured his *Memoirs of the Life of the Late John Mytton, Esq.*, with punctilious remorse. Yet, so extraordinary a hell-raiser was Mytton, that to apologize properly for his career would be near impossible.

From an early age, five bottles of the very best port constituted his morning's enjoyment, and on two occasions at least, portless, he swilled bottles of eau-de-Cologne in order to 'forestall the bad effect of night air'. Later, port having no recognizable effect, he shifted to brandy and quicksilver, thus accelerating his

Getting DOWN with no certainty of getting UP, I have an IDEA that this is the most important and effective fall, *a humorous print by Henry Alken.* '*It would do for Mytton*' *shortly became a common answer to whether a certain sort of fence or ditch could be jumped or whether any man would hazard it.*

own demise, though doubtless infusing countless bastions against the bad effect of night air. In a matter of fifteen years his expenditure on drink amounted to half a million pounds.

In an age of extreme dandyism, the Squire managed, through careful lavish-ness, to exceed all but the most finical in the matter of dress. 'An examination of his wardrobe once resulted in the discovery of a hundred and fifty-two pairs of breeches and trousers, with coats and waistcoats in proportion, seven hundred pairs of boots and slippers, over a thousand hats, nearly 3,000 shirts.' Yet, it must be noted, the various financial crises of his life must not be thought of as being directly attributable to personal extravagance, for the Squire of Halston was the very soul of generosity and kindhearted to a fault.

On the subject of his frolics, 'Nimrod' informs us, truly, that 'scarcely a day passed over his head in which he did not put his life to the hazard'. In the saddle he ran prodigious risks for his life, not only by riding with hounds at arrantly impracticable fences, but in falling from his horses when intoxicated. It shortly became a common answer to the question of whether a certain sort of fence could be leaped or whether any man would hazard it: 'it would do for Mytton'. Once he galloped full-tilt over a rabbit-warren in order to find out whether or not his horse would fall, which of course it did, rolling over him.

110

Learning, from a palpably shaky friend sitting beside him in a trap, that he had never been upset on wheels, Mytton exclaimed in astonishment: 'What! *never* upset in a gig! What a dammed slow fellow you must have been all your life!' Promptly, therefore, Mytton drove into a steep bank bordering the road and upset the trap. No real injury.

Once, in order to tickle his guests, he appeared in the drawing-room at Halston in complete hunting costume, mounted on a bear. All went well (guests fainting

The Oaks Filley *by Henry Alken. This shows Mytton under a horse surrounded by onlookers. He had bragged that when his horse won the Oaks, she would be clever enough to put the prize money into his pocket, and, to prove that she was an exceptional horse, he lay down underneath her and put her hind foot into his pocket.*

in all directions) until, signally piqued by a touch of the spur, the bear turned on his rider and ate part of his leg. This same bear, in conjunction with two bulldogs, on another occasion failed equally to be amused when forced to share a bed with a famous and drunken Shropshire horse-dealer, who died soon after. This man had probably been tiresome during the course of the evening and had suffered from Mytton's normal method with bores, which consisted in the secretion of red-hot coals in their pockets.

In the case of another horse-dealer, a cheat, Mytton was very successful in a strange attempt to secure medical attention. Handing the horse-dealer a note to a Shrewsbury banker, he instructed the man to go there and collect his money. Opening the letter, the banker – who was also the governor of the nearest lunatic asylum – found it contained the following laconic injunction, signed by Mytton: 'Admit bearer, George Underhill, into the Lunatic Asylum.'

Mytton loved to fuss and fight, even though he avoided all knowledge of self-defence. Once he fought, and beat badly, a Welsh miner who had annoyed one of the Squire's hounds by hopping about. After trouncing him over twenty rounds, the miner shouting *fin*, Mytton gave him a sum of money and instructed him to proceed to Halston 'and get *another* bellyfull'.

He didn't care about weather, and he never seemed to trust underclothing and hated shoes outdoors. Still, he never allowed the coldest water to check his progress in the pursuit of game, and he was often seen after wildfowl, lying in deep snow, wearing nothing but a shirt. Better, at his uncle's place at Woodhouse, he went out naked on to heavy ice after duck. Similarly, to win a bet with a friend over who could get home the earlier, he drove his favourite horse Baronet through Halston Lake, preferring to go as the crow flies. Again with Baronet, returning from hunting in a thoroughly frozen state, he begged relief at an unfamiliar house where he and his horse, in order to warm themselves, wrestled with each other before a large fire, which Mytton had ordered for the purpose, before proceeding on their way again.

That he loved his animals is more vividly illustrated still by another example. Frozen entirely once more, he and his horse Sportsman put up for the night at Weston-super-Mare's best hostelry, sharing throughout the night several cases of mulled port. He owned over sixty cats, and he dressed each of them in a kind of livery suitable to their breed. Dogs he did adore. A favourite bulldog was once involved in a fray in his drawing-room with another's pet. When it looked as if Tizer, Mytton's own, might come out second, his master seized the offending brute by the nose in his own jaws, until the sad creature, to all intents and purposes, resigned. The author has it, from one who asserts an ancestral kinship with

Shrewsbury from the Severn, *1845, an etching by Smyth. Mytton, early in life, came into a large fortune which included his ancestral home of Halston, near Shrewsbury, as well as an extensive estate in North Wales.*

Mytton's prominent neighbours, that Mytton kept at one point some two thousand dogs and fed most of them on champagne and beefsteak.

That the Squire had no very nice respect for his own digestion is pretty well established. He craved filberts for certain. Upon being informed that a blend of filberts and port had often been known to prove fatal, he removed a tray of filberts and a case of port to another room, and devoured the entire quantity in a few minutes, in order, as he reported, 'to clear the decks'. During one summer he had delivered to Halston two large cartloads of filberts and seven wagons of wine.

His crowning act of folly was to set fire to himself in order to banish a fit of hiccups and at the same time to demonstrate his indifference to pain. Burned to the bone in several places, and, by the way, at the point of death, his only comment, rowdily exclaimed, was: 'Well, the hiccup is gone, by God'.

And so that is how one of Nature's most remarkable men passed from life at the early age of thirty-eight, *anno domini* 1834.

113

William Beckford of Fonthill Abbey

*Shall I tell you my dreams? To give an account of my time is
doing, I assure you, but little better . . . Be content with my
visionary way of gazing*

Introducing William Beckford's travel letters written from Europe in 1780,
which he prepared for publication in 1783 under the title *Dreams, Waking
Thoughts and Incidents*, was this confession of romance. A highly personal account
of his travels, it was prophetic of the course his life was to take, where dreams,
waking thoughts and events were often fused into one.

Beckford adopted a very individual and imaginative approach to the wonders
of the European Tour, which so affronted his family that he was restrained from
publishing the book. They felt that such dark descriptions as 'the diabolical
collection of imps whispering, I warrant ye, filthy stories in his ear', of Breughel's
version of St Anthony in Hell, were no asset to any future career.

The Tour provided many contrasts, which engraved themselves on his personality: the oppressive mystery of the Bavarian mountains, the panorama of
Venice with its palaces, towers and vistas, the melancholy of the Boboli Gardens,
to name but a few. The effect of these, the introduction to monastic life at the
Grande Chartreuse in Savoy, which he visited in 1778, and an exclusive and
pampered upbringing, found Beckford at the age of twenty-one charged with a
vivid imagination and a deep sense of the romantic. His visionary gaze was to
inspire over the next sixty-three years creations of unparalleled romance. Towers
aspiring to heady heights, cutting daring silhouettes, were essential to his three
major achievements, the novel *Vathek*, the foundation of Fonthill Abbey and
the folly at Lansdown, all of which were conceived in defiance of the Age of
Reason.

William Beckford (1760–1844), *a water-colour by C. F. Taylor of Bath of the romantic novelist and builder of Fonthill Abbey.*

View of the West and South Fronts of Fonthill Abbey, *after a drawing by G. Cattermole. The architect James Wyatt was employed at Fonthill, but it is probably to Beckford himself that the scale and fancifulness is due. The tower, vying in height with the spire of Salisbury Cathedral, was inspired by Batalha, the monastery which Beckford visited in Spain. The Abbey, no longer in existence, displayed a romanticism never aspired to in architecture again, implemented by a man of genius, wild imagination and wealth.*

The novel *Vathek*, a highly coloured tale of Oriental wonder, written in French, was a brilliant work for a young man of twenty-one. Incidents in Beckford's own life were reflected and the central figure, the Caliph Vathek, was almost inseparable from Beckford himself, the Caliph of Fonthill. They both suffered from domineering, over-indulgent mothers. Carathis, Vathek's mother, contrived scenes of black magic and debauchery far in extreme of anything Mrs Beckford could envisage; however, Mrs Beckford relentlessly manipulated events in pursuing political ambitions for her son.

Alderman Beckford, a successful businessman and twice Lord Mayor of London, died when the boy was ten, leaving him a millionaire. Nothing but the best was provided for him, including piano lessons from the youthful Mozart

116

Beckford on horseback *with Lansdown Tower, Bath, in the background, a drawing by Lucius Gahagan. This is possibly a sketch for an equestrian statue of Beckford, a project that would have been quite in character with his grandiose building enterprises.*

and instruction in architecture from Sir William Chambers. Chatham became his guardian and recognized in the boy a genius he called 'all fire and air'.

Every advantage would seem to have been laid at his feet, but the over-indulged child lacked emotional outlets. Consequently, when he found a confidante in the water-colourist, Alexander Cozens, he was wide open to influence. Cozens introduced his young and impressionable pupil to mysteries of Eastern mythology and the exotic world of the *Arabian Nights*. Here lay the whole background to the romantic novel *Vathek*.

In 1777, Beckford met, while staying with the Courtneys at Powderham, young William Courtney (Kitty). That he was devoted to the boy cannot be doubted, but their relationship gave rise to malicious gossip which ultimately barred Beckford from polite society. Louisa Beckford, the wife of William Beckford's cousin, invited to Fonthill to distract William from Kitty, introduced her degenerate morals into Beckford's world; both she and Courtney played key roles in the novel. Courtney became Goulchenrouz, an innocent young boy whose arranged marriage to Nouronihar (Louisa) was shattered by the advent of the redoubtable Vathek. Goulchenrouz was left in idyllic fields of innocence, while Vathek and Nouronihar pursued the fatal search for the underground palace of the Arabian Satan, Eblis. They were drawn into the depths of debauchery and vice to join the ranks of the wicked whose burning hearts kept them in eternal purgatory.

The exotic feasts in which they participated recall a party given by Beckford in 1781 for his closest friends. Those gathered immured themselves in Fonthill House and for three days continued in endless celebrations. Never a ray of light entered their halls and the secrecy further enflamed the rumours of black magic and dabblings in the occult which came to be associated with Beckford. Years later Beckford recalled the scene:

> I still feel warm and irradiated by the recollection of that strange necromantic light which Loutherbourg had thrown over what absolutely appeared to be realms of Fairy or rather perhaps a demon temple beneath the earth, set apart for tremendous mysteries, and yet how soft, how genial was the light, it was in short a realisation of romance in the most extravagant intensity.

Between the writings of *Vathek* and the birth of Fonthill lay ten years, years which were to change the course of William Beckford's life. His risqué relationships were a source of endless concern to his mother. Matrimony seemed to be his only salvation, and Beckford was prevailed upon to co-operate. In 1783 he married Lady Margaret Gordon.

Beckford seemed set on the road to respectability, with the prospect of a peerage, when the Powderham scandal broke in 1784. He was accused of misconduct with William Courtney. The charges, although never substantiated, spelt doom to any establishment career. Margaret stood by him valiantly, but Beckford was ostracized, and life in England became intolerable. The young couple retired to Switzerland, where Margaret died in childbirth in the summer of 1786 leaving Beckford with two daughters.

This tragedy, heaped on his many other problems, might have destroyed a lesser man than Beckford. Hounded out of England and living on the Continent, he periodically indulged his melancholy but, more constructively, became an

LEFT: Frontispiece of 'Vathek' *by William Beckford from the 1834 edition published by Richard Bentley of New Burlington Street, London. 'Vathek' is a highly coloured tale of Oriental wonder with incidents drawn from Beckford's own life. The Caliph Vathek, the hero of the novel, is indistinguishable from Beckford himself.*
RIGHT: Lord Nelson's reception at Fonthill *from 'The Gentleman's Magazine', 1801, recording Beckford's one great celebration at Fonthill. It was an attempt to re-enter Society following the charge, though unsubstantiated, of misconduct.*

avid collector, tasting the flavour of flamboyant architecture in Spain and Portugal. A particularly memorable event was his extravagant expedition with the Portuguese Prince Regent and his retinue to the monasteries of Alcobaça and Batalha, where Beckford sampled monastic feasting and entertainment on the most lavish scale.

Beckford at this period lived in isolation from English society, relying mainly on his trusted staff. The social whirl of his former life was over. He no longer graced elegant soirées and entertained by his wit and singing. On his return to England, Beckford took to his estate, where he conceived the most romantic and visionary plan. He began by building a vast wall around the periphery of the main part of the estate, with the intention of repelling the huntsmen, a move hardly likely to endear him to his sporting neighbours.

> The wall is not quite so high or so long as that of China, but better built I dare say. Vathek, you will recollect, was spoilt by Carathis, and will have his way tho' it lead to the devil. In the process of time, when my hills are completely blackened with fire, I shall retreat into the centre of this gloomy circle . . . There will I build my tower and deposit my books and my writings and brood over them 'till it please Heaven to close my eyes on this strange medley of mischievous Beings and open the doors to a pleasanter existence.

Herein are the seeds of Fonthill Abbey. . . .

Beckford's dwarf. *Rumours about Beckford were rife and his one dwarf was exaggerated to a whole troop.*

Vathek had built himself a luxurious palace with five wings to appeal to each of the senses. At Fonthill, Beckford conceived a strange religious palace bearing the trappings of medieval Gothic, but planned in a chaotic fashion and appearing to the uninitiated more like a series of lengthy and uninhabitable corridors than an abbey. Nothing on this scale had ever been contemplated in England, gothic designs having previously been purely fanciful. To implement his scheme, Beckford employed the fashionable architect, James Wyatt, who had already produced several gothic essays. How much of Fonthill is Wyatt's, how much Beckford's design, is difficult to judge. However, to Beckford can certainly be attributed the grandeur and scale of the Abbey.

Fonthill Abbey after the tower collapsed, *in December 1825, engraved by Buckler. It was bad workmanship that caused the tower to fall, partly attributable to the pressure exerted on the workmen by Beckford. His enthusiasm was such that they worked at night by the light of flares.*

Initially, the building was to be a folly, a ruined convent, where Beckford could retire at leisure. The central tower and two wings appeared as the first part of the scheme. The tower, like the lofty tower to which Vathek and his mother withdrew, was the central feature. It was octagonal, inspired by Batalha, the monastery which Beckford visited, and of which Wyatt knew; in height it vied with Salisbury Cathedral spire. Sited as it was on an eminence, it provoked endless curiosity. The tall octagon, with its high pointed arches, was entered through the great west door and the western hall, an awe-inspiring chamber with a ponderous hammer-beam roof and a statue of his father, known in Beckford's jesting way, as 'the Commendatore'. The grounds were carefully contrived to give the impression of controlled but romantic natural beauty, the Bitham Lake and the thick fir woods giving a sense of Germanic oppression, hiding in their darkness unknown wonders. Beckford visited the estate each day on horseback, and when once he had voiced a scheme, droves of workmen descended on the job immediately, so that it should be complete by the next visitation, the unpredictable and violent temper of their lord and master thus being avoided.

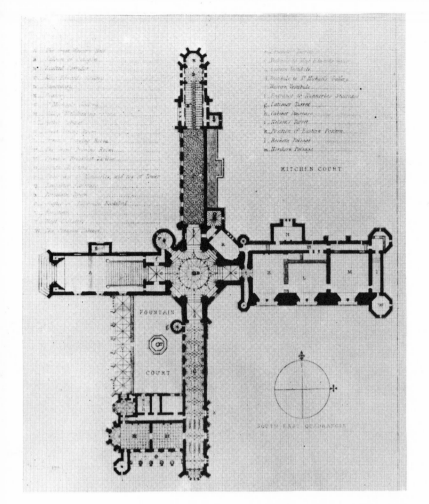

LEFT: Plan of Fonthill Abbey. *The great halls, and the octagon and galleries were decorated in ostentatious and dazzling colours which, combined with the scale of this fantastic edifice, produced a sensational effect.*

RIGHT: Lansdown Tower, Bath, *built by Beckford as his final imaginative essay in architecture, a drawing by Willes Maddox of 1844.*

To walk from these grounds into the heady romance of the Abbey must have been like walking through the looking-glass. The great halls, the octagon and galleries were all decorated in ostentatious and dazzling colours, red, gold and purple prevailing. The effect was sensational. Beckford was the Abbot and the folly was transformed by the addition of two further wings to his dwelling-place, albeit of a very impractical nature. There were numerous bedrooms, but nearly all were dark and ill-ventilated. Beckford occupied a bedroom of extreme simplicity, a striking contrast with the rest of the Abbey.

Soon after it was built the great tower collapsed as a result of shoddy workmanship. It was partly Wyatt's fault, and partly Beckford's, whose impetuosity drove the builders beyond their limits. When the pressure was greatest, gangs of workmen laboured day and night to the inconstant light of flares. Small wonder that vital foundations were omitted. Undaunted by the setbacks, Beckford rebuilt the tower.

Beckford had several friends, including the Chevalier Franchi, with whom he corresponded endlessly, in scathing tones. Everyone had a nickname: the dilatory Wyatt became known as 'Bagasse, the whoremonger', due to his failing for females; the Earl of Bridgewater, who to Beckford's chagrin made demands on Wyatt's time, would not have been flattered by the distortion of his name to 'Bilgewater'. Also of the Abbey household were the Abbé Macquin, the doctor and Beckford's dwarf. Rumours often exaggerated the one dwarf to a whole troop, with the attributes of Vathek's eunuchs.

Beckford hated to see animals harmed and his love for them perhaps compensated for the absence of his family. Certainly his dogs, Caroline, Nephew and Viscount Fartleberry, were devoted companions. The year 1800 saw Fonthill's one great celebration and Beckford's final attempt to return to the social scene, though he still shunned his hunting neighbours. He invited Lord Nelson, Sir William and Lady Hamilton, the renowned Emma, with suitable companions. The guests stayed at Fonthill House, but the banquet was staged at the Abbey. The party was driven through the Fonthill estate after being welcomed by the Fonthill volunteers. Lights blazed through the woods and a visitor recorded:

> The Company on their arrival at the Abbey could not fail to be struck with the increasing splendour of the lights and their effects, contrasted with the deep shades that fell upon the walls and battlements and arches of the great tower, till it vanished by degrees into an awful gloom at its summit.

The assembled company was entertained to a lavish feast in the manner of ancient abbeys. Dinner was followed by an entertainment: mysterious hooded figures with large wax torches lit the way to King Edward's Gallery, where St Anthony's shrine was revealed and mysterious music emanated from an invisible quarter. The pageant also included Lady Hamilton in one of her famous 'attitudes', her choice for Fonthill being Agrippina presenting the ashes of Germanicus to the Roman people, a scene she conveyed so poignantly that tears ran down the spectators' cheeks. The company left the strange nocturnal scene at eleven o'clock and drove home through the estate. 'They passed the sacred boundary of the great wall as if waking from a dream or just freed from the influence of some magic spell.'

Beckford's intentions were not entirely altruistic. The desire for a peerage still dogged him and, through Emma's good offices, he tried to enlist Sir William's support, but he received a cold rebuff from that quarter.

This glamorous occasion was the only one of its kind staged by Beckford. He

Frontispiece of 'Vathek', *from the first edition, written in French and published in 1815. The turbanned eye from which radiate shafts of light anticipates the mystery and originality of the novel, written when the author was twenty-one.*

moved permanently into the Abbey in 1807, where he continued to indulge his acquisitive instincts. Although isolation was self-inflicted, he was lonely and often unhappy. His eldest daughter married much against his will, and only his younger daughter's betrothal to the Duke of Hamilton's eldest son pleased him and revived the hope of influential string-pulling for a peerage. He once remarked: 'Some people drink to forget their unhappiness; I build.' The megalomaniac building activity at Fonthill betrays the sensitive side of his personality.

In the early nineteenth century he began to suffer financially owing to the slump in the sugar market, the source of his wealth. Despite his accountant's warning he continued to collect books and pictures. He had a connoisseur's knowledge, but his attitude was that of a pure dilettante; he acquired indiscriminately in all fields of art. Shortage of cash finally forced him to sell Fonthill, which he did with cavalier sang-froid. The Abbey was opened for view, and thousands flocked to ogle at this eccentric man's creation, for so long a forbidden realm. Characteristically, Beckford snubbed Christie's and sold the Abbey and its contents to a private bidder at the eleventh hour and on his final morning tour of the grounds he gave instructions for some immediate changes, causing gardeners to scurry from all quarters in a fever of activity. Then he returned to the house, entered his coach and set off for Bath, never to return. Two years after he left, the tower collapsed finally, and so vanished the greatest of his visions.

Viscount Fartleberry, *Beckford's dog, drawn by Abbé Macquin.*

Beckford was the cause of much curiosity in the gossip-ridden spa, his reputation preceding him, and he in turn did all he could to foster it by a parade of eccentricity. He moved into two houses in Lansdown Crescent, which flanked the entrance to a mews; the linking bridge room, built by Beckford, still exists. Soon after he purchased a third house in the crescent, an extravagant gesture he explained away with the words:

> Now had I not bought this house I should have been perpetually annoyed by the ticking of some cursed jack, the jingling of some beastly piano, horrid toned bells tinkling and so on. The only way to avoid this was by buying the house; and so I bought it to the infinite annoyance and astonishment of the Bath aristocracy, an odd breed I believe.

Into these houses he introduced his most favoured possessions, and he continued to do business with his bookseller, Clarke, nicknamed Boletus (mushroom) because of his large head and short neck and body.

Beckford was not long content without a tower. For this final adventure, he employed a young Bath architect to design a retreat for him, at the end of a tract of land he had leased along the brow of Lansdown. Henry Goodridge produced a number of designs, including a gothic lighthouse, but Beckford changed his stylistic tune and chose a design in the then fashionable Graeco-Roman manner. So his final tower rose up more solidly rooted in the ground than his former enterprise, and it still stands as a memorial to him today. Between the tower and the house he laid out extensive gardens, importing fully grown trees, and transforming the barren hillside into a charmed wilderness. The mysteries of *Vathek* still persisted in the old man's imagination. He was much flattered when a visitor compared his entrance hall with the Hall of Eblis. 'You are right', Beckford observed, gazing at the draped curtains and the view down a distant passage, 'this is unquestionably the Hall of Eblis.'

William Beckford died in Bath with his daughter, the Duchess of Hamilton, by his side. His body was placed in a costly granite sarcophagus made according to his instructions. The funeral procession, the last spectacle of his own creation, witnessed as always by crowds of people, was composed of his family and retainers, all dressed in costumes specially commissioned for the occasion, with an immense plume held high over the coffin. Some years later, the Duchess gave Lansdown tower and grounds as an extension to the parish churchyard, and Beckford finally came to rest at the foot of his last romantic folly.

William Beckford never conformed to the accepted rules of society. He lived to his own code, regardless of those around him, and throughout his turbulent life he excited much speculation. The diarist, Lord Farington, quoted Fuseli as saying, 'he is an actor but not a gentleman'. Horace Walpole disdained him as an upstart, and it is unlikely that the Fonthill Gothic would have accorded with Walpole's own version of the Gothic. To romantics he was a prophet. Fonthill bridged the gap between the playful Strawberry Hill Gothic and the serious nineteenth-century vision of the Gothic Revival. The Abbey displayed romantic heights never aspired to again, implemented by a man of genius, wild imagination and wealth, and the effects were sensational both to the contemporary visitor and to the later gothic enthusiast. Disraeli called him 'the man of the greatest taste'. If this is difficult to stomach, he was certainly a man of the greatest vision, and maintained to his death, and after, an aura of wonder. His life was a romantic *tour de force*, shrouded in deep mystery. It could still be said of him in 1838 that he was 'the formidable and inaccessible Vathek himself'.

Julia Margaret Cameron

'Is there *nobody* here who is commonplace?', cried a commonplace young woman who was visiting Freshwater, in the Isle of Wight, about a hundred years ago. Possibly not, for the little colony there which circled round Tennyson, living 'in a radiance of mutual admiration', included the painter G. F. Watts, Thackeray's two daughters, the Thoby Prinseps and the Charles Camerons, and was constantly enlivened by a *va-et-vient* of their distinguished intellectual friends. None of these was commonplace, but one alone could be classed as an eccentric: Julia Margaret Cameron – chiefly remembered today for her pioneer work as a photographer.

Julia was the second of the seven famous Pattle sisters, daughters of a rich Anglo-Indian named James Pattle – known to his friends as 'Jim Blazes' and to his enemies as 'the greatest liar in India' – and his French wife, both long since dead. The third daughter, Sarah (Mrs Prinsep), was known as 'Dash'; the sixth, Virginia (Lady Somers), as 'Beauty'; and Julia, the brilliant ugly duckling, very properly as 'Talent'.

The Tennysons were the first to arrive at Freshwater, where in 1853 they rented, and subsequently bought, a large, late Georgian house, Farringford. In 1860 they were joined by Charles Cameron – described by Tennyson as a 'philosopher with his beard dipped in moonlight' – and his wife, who converted three cottages into a house which they named 'Dimbola' after one of their estates in Ceylon. Cameron was at this time sixty-five, his wife twenty years younger. Freshwater in those days was still remote. The railway had not yet reached it, and visitors were conveyed there in a two-horse coach from Yarmouth, where on their return they were directed to the steamer with a cry of 'This way for England!' Tennyson became, of course, the principal attraction; but Mrs Cameron was the colony's stage manager. Mary Watts, the artist's second wife, wrote that she 'baffled description', possessing a double share of all those qualities (except beauty) which made the Pattle family so exceptional; and Benjamin Jowett, for whom she built a little cottage nearby, described her as 'a very honest, really kind, enthusiastic person: perhaps she has a tendency to make the house shake the moment she enters, but in this dull world that is a very excusable fault'. She could also shake chapels,

The Annunciation. *A highly romanticized representation of this Biblical incident taken, as Julia Margaret Cameron expressed it, 'From Life', in 1865 at Freshwater. The young sitter was her great-niece Laura Gurney, later Lady Troubridge, who recalled the incident saying 'Our roles were no less than those of two angels of the Nativity and to sustain them we were scantily clad, and each had a pair of heavy swan's wings fastened to our narrow shoulders, while Aunt Julia, with ungentle hand, tousled our hair to get rid of its prim nursery look'.*

and Lady Ritchie (Thackeray's daughter) recalls an embarrassing occasion when she blew kisses throughout the sermon to that distinguished preacher, the Rev. William Brookfield, at the Berkeley Chapel in Mayfair.

The Return after Three Days. *A singularly healthy looking child, possibly again the eight-year-old Laura Gurney, is photographed after having just returned to her family after an absence of three days.*

Mrs Cameron was wildly generous. Her friend the poet Sir Henry Taylor, a regular visitor to Dimbola, who with his wife 'suffered the extreme fury of her affection', wrote, 'She keeps showering on us her "barbaric pearls and gold", Indian shawls, turquoise bracelets, inlaid portfolios, ivory elephants'. Nor might gifts be refused. When on one occasion Lady Taylor sent back a particularly valuable shawl, Mrs Cameron sold it and with the proceeds bought an expensive invalid sofa which she presented in Lady Taylor's name to the Putney Hospital for Incurables. 'Julia is slicing up Ceylon', poor old Cameron would say – half sorrowfully, half admiringly – when he found his wife embarking on yet another extravagance.

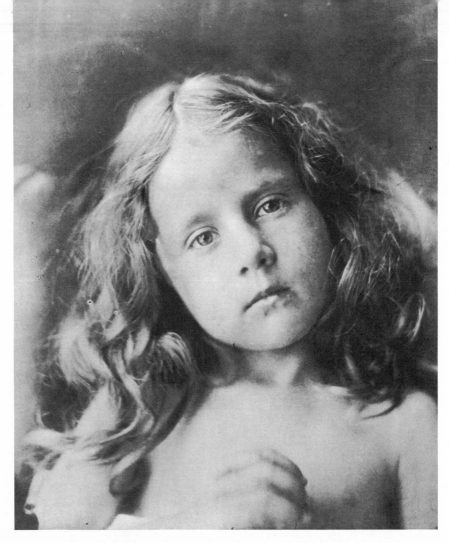

The Anniversary, *a wistful birthday photograph of a young girl, supporting Mrs Cameron's contention that no woman should ever allow herself to be photographed between the age of eighteen and eighty.*

The turning-point in Mrs Cameron's life came when in 1863 her daughter Julia gave her a camera. Portrait photography now became an obsession. She turned her coal-cellar into a dark-room, her fowl-house into a studio, working 'fruitlessly but not hopelessly . . . to arrest all the beauty that came before me'. 'Arrest' is the operative word. From her window, which overlooked the path down to the landing-stage of the ferry, she would watch for the arrival of photogenic victims, and anyone who attracted her was immediately pounced on and kidnapped for her by one of her maids, and compelled to pose motionless for what seemed like hours on end. 'Her sitters came at her summons', wrote Lady Ritchie. 'They trembled, or would have trembled, could they have dared, when the round black eye of the camera was turned upon them. They felt what consequences, what disastrous waste of time and money and effort might ensue from any passing quiver of emotion'.

Pray God, bring Father Safely Home; *the young girl prays to her mother for the safe return of her father. Julia Margaret Cameron's relations and the local cottagers were frequently pressed into co-operating over her photographic tableaux. This example is intended to illustrate 'Three Fishers set sailing out into the Deep' by the great Victorian poet and novelist, Charles Kingsley (1819–75).*

Besides those unknown captives unwittingly immortalized by Mrs Cameron there were, of course, the famous who were cajoled or bullied into posing. Old Sir Henry Taylor, whom she idolized in a manner bordering on the ridiculous and referred to as 'my peculiar friend', was constantly victimized. 'I don't see

A Self Portrait *of the photographer as an older woman, who was described by Mary Watts, the artist's second wife, as 'baffling description' and possessing a double share of all those qualities (except beauty) which made the Pattle family so exceptional.*

what you mean by his extraordinary beauty', Tennyson once cried after he had been subjected to yet another exhausting eulogy of Taylor; 'why, he had a smile like a fish'. 'Only when the Spirit of the Lord moved on the face of the waters, Alfred', replied Mrs Cameron.

Tennyson, though a reluctant sitter, was also made to pose innumerable times, and at his suggestion she made a series of illustrations for *The Idylls of the King*, for which all and sundry, including complete strangers, were pressed into service. The Yarmouth porter proved an admirable King Arthur, and his Guinevere was a girl abducted on the beach. It was Tennyson who brought Longfellow to the torture-chamber, leaving him there with the words, 'You will have to do whatever she tells you. I will come back soon and see what is left of you.' Rossetti, the bravest man in all England, alone refused to obey her summons, but Browning was another and a terrified victim. Abandoned in a posture of extreme discomfort while the absent-minded photographer went off in search of some missing piece of equipment, he was not remembered and rescued, more dead than alive, until some two hours later.

So keen was Mrs Cameron to photograph Garibaldi, who had come to visit Tennyson, that she rushed to Farringford, fell on her knees at his feet and, being innocent of Italian, made a gesture of supplication; but Garibaldi, mistaking her for some old beggar-woman who had strayed into his host's garden, brushed her aside. Darwin – the only sitter known to have *paid* for being immortalized – inscribed beneath his portrait, 'I like this photograph very much better than any other which has been taken of me', and Carlyle commented on his, 'It is as if suddenly the picture began to speak, terrifically ugly and woe-begone, but has something of a likeness: my candid opinion' Watts wrote on receiving a batch of her recent work, 'All the heads are divine, and the plates very nearly perfect.'

'No woman', wrote Mrs Cameron, 'should ever allow herself to be photographed between the age of eighteen and eighty.' There were always young people about the place, and one of these, her great-niece Laura Gurney (Lady Troubridge), was later to leave a most valuable account of this formidable yet fascinating creature as seen through the eyes of a very sophisticated eight-year old:

> To me, I frankly own, she appeared as a terrifying elderly woman, short and squat, with none of the Pattle grace and beauty about her, though more than her share of their passionate energy and wilfulness. Dressed in dark clothes, stained with chemicals from her photography (and smelling of them, too), with a plump, eager face and piercing eyes and a voice husky, and a little harsh, yet in some ways compelling and even charming, my first sight of her was in her studio at Dimbola . . . and immediately we, Rachel [her sister] and I, were pressed into the service of the camera. Our *rôles* were no less than those of two of the angels of the Nativity, and to sustain them we were scantily clad, and each had a pair of heavy swan's wings fastened to her narrow shoulders, while Aunt Julia, with ungentle hand, tousled our hair to get rid of its prim nursery look.
>
> No wonder those old photographs of us, leaning over imaginary ramparts of heaven, look anxious and wistful. This is how we felt, for we never knew what Aunt Julia was going to do next, nor did anyone else for the matter of that. All we were conscious of was that once in her clutches we were perfectly helpless. 'Stand there', she shouted. And we stood for hours, if necessary, gazing at the model of the Heavenly Babe (in reality a sleeping child deposited in a property manger). The parents, anxious and uneasy, were outside, no more able to rescue their infant until Aunt Julia had finished with it, than we should have been.

The Whisper of the Muse, *a sentimental photograph of the painter George Frederic Watts (1817–1904) flanked by two spirits of the muse. G. F. Watts was a member of the artistic and intellectual Freshwater colony on the Isle of Wight where the inner circle 'lived in a radiance of mutual admiration'.*

One of Mrs Cameron's self-appointed tasks was that of making the Laureate behave. When he refused, during a smallpox scare, to be vaccinated, she brought the doctor and his lymph to Farringford and shouted, 'Alfred, you're a coward!' until the great man yielded. When he refused to receive three American admirers who had made the pilgrimage to see the bard, she burst with them into his house crying, 'Alfred! These gentlemen have come from afar to see the British *Lion*,

Alfred, Lord Tennyson (1809–92), *a photograph of the poet taken when he was aged sixty and Poet Laureate of ten years standing. Tennyson, the principal member of the Freshwater colony, though a reluctant sitter, was made to pose innumerable times and at his suggestion Julia Margaret Cameron made a series of illustrations for 'The Idylls of the King' for which all and sundry, including complete strangers were pressed into service.*

and behold a *Bear*!' And no doubt it was she who saw to it that each, when they came to leave, received a signed copy of the *Idylls*.

Like everything associated with Mrs Cameron, her departure from Dimbola was dramatic and improbable. Yet it would seem that it was not she but her husband – the invalid and more or less housebound octogenarian – who in the autumn of 1875 suddenly took the wild decision to return to Ceylon to join several of his sons who were looking after the family's coffee plantations there. But Mrs Cameron readily acquiesced: 'Where your heart is', she told Laura, 'there is your treasure also.'

Mary Fraser-Tytler (the future Mrs Watts), a visitor to Freshwater that autumn, has described the events that followed: 'The striking of the tents of the Cameron household was full of characteristic unusualness – Mrs Cameron providing for every contingency possible, to the point of unconscious humour. The house was soon in a state of turmoil, their rooms piled up with packing-cases, while telegrams poured in and out, and friends came in crowds to say their farewell. All Freshwater was wailing! Rich and poor . . .'

Among the contingencies provided for was death, Mrs Cameron including among her baggage two coffins (filled temporarily with china and glass) to ensure decent burial should she and her husband never return; and possibly the 'unconscious humour' was also supplied by the cow that led the procession up the gangway when they embarked. Mary was not at Southampton to see them sail; but she was told that almost the whole of Freshwater was, and that since Mrs Cameron had by then run out of ready money she was to be seen showering the porters with large mounted photographs of Carlyle in lieu of tips, saying as she did so, 'Take this instead as a remembrance!'

The voyage was without incident. From some port of call Mrs Cameron wrote to Lady Tennyson: 'I need not tell you that amidst all this bustling world of 380 people, my husband sits in majesty like a being from another sphere, his white hair shining like the foam of the sea and his white hands holding on each side of his golden chain . . .' To mark her gratitude for their safe arrival at Colombo, she collected enough money from the passengers to purchase a harmonium for the ship's captain. Of course she had brought her camera with her, and in the *Recollections of a Happy Life* by Marianne North, a woman in many ways almost as remarkable as herself who was at that time painting the flora of Ceylon, we are able to catch a last glimpse of Mrs Cameron at work. 'She made me stand with spiky coconut branches running into my head', Miss North wrote, 'and told me to look perfectly natural.'

The coffins had not been brought in vain. Mrs Cameron died in 1879, the splendour of the Ceylon hillsides spread before her eyes, and the word 'Beautiful' was the last to pass her lips. A year later her husband followed her to the grave, and that other Dimbola at Freshwater, once a place of so much wonder, is now in part a boarding-house.

Algernon Charles Swinburne

Algernon Charles Swinburne (1837–1909) was of impeccable lineage. In him the blue blood of the Ashburnhams and Swinburnes merged to form a dubious little republican. He was born with the 'eyes of a god and the smile of an elf'. From the outset of his life appearances gave him away, and even the best education which Victorian England could provide only rendered it impossible to find another man brought up at Eton and Oxford 'who continued so unlike all other human beings'.

Spanning the Victorian century, in touch with the greatest literary minds on both sides of the Channel, reviled and revered in his own time, he was something the Victorians could never understand or tolerate: not a booming-voiced poet of the Tennysonian variety, but a genuine eccentric, utterly unable to cope with the stuffy plush morality of the time, although he was perverted and transformed by it.

Eton made an extraordinary impression on Swinburne. He arrived 'strangely tiny and defenceless, his body far too weak to carry his great head, the size of which was exaggerated by the tousled mass of red hair standing almost at right angles to it'. Lord Redesdale's description was prophetic: his body was too weak to support his huge head. The contrast of the fine, beautifully chiselled features and the flaming aggressive hair symbolized very neatly the inward conflict which marked Algernon from his compatriots, budding Empire builders every one.

Even as a child, other children could discern the over-mothered, hyper-sensitive species which would not, could not, ever break into adulthood. Clutching his 'Bowdler's' Shakespeare, burying himself in Froissart's chronicles, Algernon was irrefutably dubbed 'shy and reserved'. But although uncategorizable, he was preserved from being thought an insufferable prig by his dignity and brand of tough courage, and also by his weird, almost monstrous, appearance. He distinguished himself by having the largest hat in the school at twelve-years-old, though after his death the size of his head was denied as it was considered obscene for a revered man of letters to have had such a freakish distinction.

At Eton, the little white face with the great aureole of flaming hair commanded respect. It undeniably takes a rare quality to be accepted by twelve-year-old

137

Algernon Charles Swinburne (1837–1909), *a photograph taken of the poet in his late twenties. Swinburne was at this period of his life living in London, where he was studying feverishly and indulging hectically in drink and the social round.*

contemporaries, when your thoughts and appearance differ radically from theirs. Swinburne had this quality: a genuine and rare eccentricity allied with poetic genius. When a friend dosing him for 'flu found a boy 'who stood up on his bed instead of lying on it and whose rolling eye accompanied a passionate outpouring of verse', he feared delirium, only to be informed, 'It's only little Swinburne reciting verse as usual'.

In spite of his weird and whimsical appearance, Swinburne did not waste time. He read voraciously and precociously. By the age of fourteen he was devoted to the minor Elizabethan and Jacobean dramatists, Shakespeare, Wordsworth and Marlowe. His friend, Lord Redesdale, gives a vivid impression of Algernon's erudition and haunting miasmic charm. ' "A" was now devouring the great classics of France and Italy. His memory was wonderful, his power of quotation almost unlimited. We used to take long walks together in Windsor Forest . . . As he walked along with that peculiar dancing step of his, his eyes gleaming with enthusiasm, and his hair like the Zazzera of the old Florentines, tossed about by the wind, he would pour out, in his unforgettable voice, the treasures which he had gathered at his last sitting'. Other boys would watch him with amazement, looking upon him as a sort of inspired elfin – something belonging to another sphere. He carried with him one magic charm – he was absolutely courageous. He did not know what fear meant.

Intellectual precocity went hand in hand with a naive 'stainless innocence'. Idyllic holidays with his family in the Isle of Wight and Northumberland spent swimming, reciting and being adored and admired by his mother and sisters, combined with a school life devouring Landor and Hugo and composing great elegiacs, sounds like a universally agreed 'earthly paradise'. Unfortunately, more sinister and macabre formative elements were creeping into Swinburne's psyche. The beatings he received at Eton were to give him a life-long addiction to correction, an affliction which found a literary outlet in *The Flogging Block*. Now preserved from public sight in the British Museum, this long poem is a sad testimonial to the effects of public school discipline. Described as a heroic poem by 'Rufus Rodworthy, Esq., with annotations by Barebum Birchingham, Esq', the whole work has been bound in blue Morocco and illustrated by Simeon Solomon. Although not essentially pornographic, there are touches of sensuality:

What a great fleshy bottom, both fleshy and brawny,
As plump as two peaches, not skinny and tawny
Like yours, you know Charlton is Featherstonehaugh's
What a field for the birch and is marked as with claws.

Cartoon for glass *by Dante Gabriel Rossetti (1828–82), poet and painter and the son of an Italian political refugee living in London. Rossetti was one of the central figures in the Pre-Raphaelite group to which Swinburne became both attracted and attached. He met Rossetti while still up at Oxford, where it is recorded that at their first meeting his physical impact was so strong that Rossetti immediately asked him to pose. Rossetti found Swinburne's lack of sexual life extremely perplexing and on another occasion thought that by posing him clutching Frances Cornforth to his bosom the compromising situation would provide him with the necessary opportunity to liaise with the opposite sex. The effect was quite the converse.*

THE EARLY ITALIAN POETS
from Ciullo d'Alcamo to Dante Alighieri
translated by D. Gabriel Rossetti.

London. Smith, Elder & Co. 1861

Golden bells or silver rolled
Never forth such notes, nor told
Hours so blithe in tones so bold
As the radiant mouth of gold
~~Here that sings forth~~
~~Raising joy like~~ heaven
If the golden-crested wren
If Were a nightingale — why, then
Something seen & heard of men
Might be half as sweet as when
Laughs a child of seven

LEFT: Frontispiece *by D. G. Rossetti for 'The Early Italian Poets', translated by D. G. Rossetti, which provided an early influence for Swinburne. This phase soon passed since Swinburne's natural taste was not for medieval poetry but for Greek and Elizabethan drama. By the time of his first published poems, he had attained a style of his own.*
RIGHT: Original draft of 'A Child's Laughter'. *An intense admirer of Shelley, this is one of Swinburne's lyrical poems which demonstrates his considerable success in this field.*

The poem is mainly concerned with the psychological reactions of the boys to one another's experience. Occasionally the work shows flashes of wit as in the chorus:

> Algernon's bottom and Birkenshaw's rod
> Ain't they a couple of lovers, by God.

The poem is best kept hidden in the British Museum, but it does give some idea of what Eton did to him. The fey creature who liked to idle away his time contemplating butterflies and seamews in the Isle of Wight had been coarsened and brutalized; his early experiences blighted and dominated his entire life. It made it impossible for him ever to have normal sexual relations and led him inexorably from the cosy intellectual haven of Oxford, down the primrose path to alcoholism, Simeon Solomon, and eventually to a claustrophobic salvation in Putney.

At Oxford Swinburne remained in his rooms. When he emerged 'there was a want of youthful freshness in his face'. However, he still walked delicately 'like Agag, with a mounting gait, as if picking his steps'. He made the conventional undergraduate gestures and he tried desperately to shake off his Ashburnham mother's influence. He renounced Christianity and took up, not with other undergraduates of similarly privileged backgrounds, but with three artists who had come to decorate the Union Society Debating Hall.

Swinburne met Burne-Jones and William Morris at a friend's rooms and they introduced him to Rossetti. His physical impact was so strong that Rossetti immediately asked him to pose. 'Dear Carrots' became absorbed in the Pre-Raphaelite principles. It was the inspiration he needed to spur his own creative impulse; he began to paint in words the pure legends and ethereal beauties he saw in their rich canvases. The Pre-Raphaelite Movement was the apotheosis of the Victorian age; it transformed, then crystalized the Victorian ethic into mouth-watering sugar plums, ready to be consumed by the proletariat. Algernon, the auburn-locked scion of a noble family, with romantically republican leanings, was the perfect expositor of their creed. But it destroyed him. He could not survive the raucously heterosexual, sensual pressures it laid on him; he was a creature of air and water, a 'pseudo Shelley', as Arnold describes him, who could not fit into the role that they assigned him.

He failed to graduate and retreated to Navestock, to friends of his parents. Although his Oxford friends realized that he was an extraordinary being, Swinburne's increasingly excitable and extravagant behaviour impressed on his tutor Jowett and his father that he should leave Oxford for the serenity of a country vicarage.

His arrival at the Stubbs' was dramatic; he arrayed himself in scarlet slippers and a crimson dressing-gown and sauntered into the vicarage garden to watch the locals going to church. The Vicar wondered why no one had arrived to worship; he went to investigate and found a 'silent swelling' crowd, too terrified to pass the flaming apparition at the gate. Poor Stubbs. When he and his wife gently criticized the amatory passages of *Rosamund, Queen of the Lombards*, they were confronted not with the modest confusion they expected, but with a long silent stare, followed by a scream which rent the vicarage, and then a bolt upstairs by the outraged genius, where he burnt the entire manuscript.

At 'The Pines' *by Max Beerbohm (1872–1956). Watts-Dunton, depicted to the right of Swinburne, was his amanuensis who removed him to his bachelor abode, 'The Pines', on Putney Hill. Here he preserved Swinburne in aspic, a curio shown only to a carefully selected public for a limited time. A pint of brown ale and regular walks to the 'Rose and Crown' produced no further rebellion.*

In London, Swinburne became a fiery comet in the Pre-Raphaelite sphere, studying feverishly and indulging hectically in drink and the social round. His sanity was kept intact by parental intervention and an enforced holiday by the Mediterranean, which he described 'as one dead flat sapphire, void of wrath' and the Riviera as the 'dullest bit of earth in Europe'. In spite of a reasonable income which enabled him to travel and indulge his leisure, Swinburne, between sensational fainting fits at the British Museum, produced the bulk of his creative work in London. The beautiful narrative poems *Chastelard*, *Atalanta in Calydon*, *Dolores* and *Faustine* poured from his pen. He managed to devour Sade, and have himself immortalized by Rossetti, clutching the loathed Fanny Cornforth to his bosom. Rossetti found Swinburne's lack of sexual life extremely perplexing and thought that by posing him in such a compromising manner he was providing him with the necessary opportunity to liaise with the opposite sex. The effect was quite the converse. Swinburne's dislike of the voluptuous, romantically inclined females, although embryonic, was sufficiently developed to direct him to the Circus Road establishment and the charms of the insidious Simeon Solomon.

A Victorian conspiracy on the part of Gosse, Beerbohm, A. E. Housman and William Rossetti to veil Swinburne's scandalous sexual activities from the prying eyes of posterity has managed to obscure his real image. When he was shown Gosse's portfolio on Algernon's vices, Beerbohm wrote: 'How definitely dreary and ghastly the whole thing becomes; why should anyone in posterity *know* Swinburne did these things?'

'These things' refer to Swinburne's visitations to a luxuriously furnished house in Circus Road, St John's Wood, where two fair-haired and rouged ladies whipped any gentleman who would pay them for their services. To contemporaries, absorbed in the delicate whimsy of Algernon's character, the thought of this neo-Platonist sprite indulging in such perversion must have been shocking. But the great eclectic mind, the genius and friend of genius, ranging from Wordsworth to Thomas Hardy, was at this time scarcely able to write a letter to a friend without extolling either the virtues of flogging or of de Sade.

Although unaffected by opinion and unchanged by conditions, he was, in a curious way, wholly dependent on others; by turn on Jowett, Burton, Rossetti and Watts-Dunton. The needle could and did swing violently between the opposite poles; Algernon's sanity and his genius relied on a dependable, benign influence. Though physically extraordinarily tough and wiry, a life of sado-masochism and endless alcohol was gradually wearing out his febrile system. A saviour was called for.

Swinburne and his sisters *by the famous society portrait painter, George Richmond. Swinburne spent idyllic holidays with his family on the Isle of Wight and in Northumberland, swimming, reciting and being adored and admired by his mother and sisters.*

Simeon Solomon started his courtship of Swinburne by letter and, from what one can gather, they had a protracted and sensual affair, on paper. Their correspondence is mainly concerned with their mutual obsession, flogging, and it benefited neither of them. Swinburne, at least, felt safe, immune from society's strictures and above all from his mother's knowledge. Solomon himself was an enigmatic man; a talented artist, he was also ambitious for literary success, but too proud to ask for assistance from his family. With truly Biblical splendour, he ended up by chalking the pavements and eventually died in the poor house. His death certificate pathetically notes his occupation as a 'painter in oils'.

Both Swinburne's closest friendships, with Dante Gabriel Rossetti and Solomon, came to grief. For post-Freudians it is almost too simple to analyze the reasons; he could only reject those who came too close; they endangered the sovereignty of his mother, radiating soft reproach from the current family home, but managing to keep the filial bond as tight as ever. Even Simeon, so handsome and so desperate to please, had to be rejected.

The 'insufferable little prig' was throwing off danger signals thick and fast: Munby, the eminent Victorian man of letters, who maintained a secret marriage with his serving girl, was constantly bumping into him at the Arts Club and gives a gloriously sober Victorian view of the *enfant terrible* of the literary hierarchy. Besides 'foaming and dancing', and kissing his fingers to illustrate 'strong delight', he waved his arms and writhed his 'little legs', was obviously drunk and proclaimed, 'Montalembert; Ohooo, it is glorious, he died damned'. One can sense Munby stiffening, whiskers shivering in horror, as Swinburne embraced Alfred Bailey, with whom he was dining in 'an insane and indecent fashion'. The committee called on Swinburne to resign.

In a more reflective moment, Munby took time to make 'this man an object of grave and pathetic study . . . he is so reckless and childish and ungovernable, so far from all sobriety and restraint, from all ordinary moral sanctions and beliefs, and yet so full of genius, of noble enthusiasm for freedom and beauty, and so genuine and kindly in his way'. The noble genius was heading for a physical and nervous breakdown, but he had found a saviour.

Watts-Dunton was a solicitor and book critic, in other words a legal man with literary pretensions. He had become Swinburne's legal adviser, and gradually, realizing his need for a realistic and practical friend, his amanuensis. It was left to Watts-Dunton to remove Swinburne bodily to his bachelor abode on Putney Hill. Here he was preserved in aspic, a curio shown only to a carefully selected public for a limited time. Although occasional flashes of wit and genius managed to permeate the over-oxygenated, damasked atmosphere of *The Pines*, the gay,

Algernon Charles Swinburne, *drawing executed in 1874 by Carlo Pellegrini.*

iconoclastic republican was extremely successfully homogenized by the rigorously healthy routine enforced by his benign gaoler. A pint of brown ale and regular walks on Wimbledon Common to the *Rose and Crown*, produced no further rebellion. He, who had the power to incite others to rebellion, was reduced to eating like a caterpillar and sleeping like a dormouse in a 'leyden jar'.

Swinburne was transformed into 'a child at play with his toys, turning for comfort, self-forgetfulness and consolation to poetry, in itself a toy'. And it was to a child that he turned for his last eccentric passionate fling, to Bertie Mason, Watts-Dunton's nephew of nine years old. Swinburne fell hopelessly in love with him and wrote endless poems, some of which even admit the odd quirk of his passion:

> But eyes of father and mother
> Like sunshine shed on you shine;
> What need you have of another
> Such new, strange love as mine.

His mother forbade anyone to make him self-conscious by reproaching him with his strange obsession, and she was right; sublimated, it gradually quietened and died.

When the Poet Laureateship became vacant on Tennyson's death, Queen Victoria commented, 'I am told that Mr Swinburne is the greatest poet in my dominion'. The rebel had achieved the ultimate accolade of respectability, Watts-Dunton had achieved complete success: Gladstone, however, chipped in that his political views made him unfit for the office.

The ultimate paradox, was that the convention-breaker, the scarlet sodomite, the tropical bird of the Pre-Raphaelites, had become a dull grey candidate for the Laureateship of Victoria's last years, writing of babies and butterflies in suburban Putney.

It took a French author, Guy de Maupassant, to capture Swinburne's essentially un-British essence: he remarked after meeting him as a young man, '*Il avait une manière de voir et comprendre, qui me le montait comme une visionaire malade, ivre de poésie, perverse et magique*'. (He had a way of seeing and understanding which revealed him to me as a sick visionary, drunk with poetry, wayward and magical.)

Romeo Coates

On 15 February, 1848, among those present at Allcroft's Grand Annual Concert was an elderly sallow-faced gentleman. Later, sitting in his carriage, he would realize he had left his opera glasses in the theatre and, as he ran back to retrieve them, would be struck down by a hansom and crushed against a passing carriage. Such would be the death, at seventy-five, of Mr Robert Coates, then living quietly in reduced but comfortable circumstances but who in his prime thirty years before had been, of all the overblown grotesques of the regency pageant, perhaps the most absurd and unfortunate, and certainly one of the most spectacular.

This was 'Diamond' Coates, whose person, in his more prosperous past, had been adorned by galaxies of gems flashing beneath the furs he wore, summer and winter alike. This too was 'Curricle' Coates, whose scallop-shaped chariot, or curricle, painted a 'beautiful rich lake colour', was once one of the sights of Long Acre. More vulgarly he had been named Mr Cockadoodle Coates, mocked for the crest he affected: a cock with outspread wings and the motto 'While I live, I'll crow'. Most notably this was 'Romeo' Coates. The gentleman himself had preferred the description, 'The Amateur of Fashion'; 'The Philanthropic Amateur' or, better still, 'The Gifted Amateur', but to the crowd he was always 'Romeo'. For what had distinguished Coates from others of his kind, had been the conviction that he could act; and especially that he could act the part of Romeo. This belief had sustained him on the stages of London, Bath and the provinces in the face of catcalls, cockcrows, hurled oranges and terrified fellow-actors, and it had made him, throughout the seasons of 1810 to 1816, one of the wonders of the fashionable world.

Born in Antigua in 1772, Coates first arrived in Bath in 1809. His father, a rich sugar-planter and merchant, had left his only surviving son £40,000 a year to squander, a fabulous collection of diamonds and a will expressly requiring that his estates should be administered by trustees and not by the heir.

Also in Bath that season was a Mr Pryse Gordon, who like Coates was staying at York House and who reports in his memoirs: 'He shortly attracted my attention by rehearsing passages of Shakespeare during his morning meal with a tone and gesture extremely striking both to the eye and ear.' Undaunted by this unusual

Robert Coates, Esq., *an engraving published in the 'European Magazine', 1 April, 1813.*

behaviour during breakfast, and noticing that Coates did not always stick to the text, Mr Gordon struck up an acquaintanceship with him and even ventured to correct Coates in a certain passage from *Romeo and Juliet*. 'Aye', said he, 'that is the reading I know, for I have the whole play by heart, but I think I have improved on it.'

Pryse Gordon soon discovered that the literary gentleman had frequently taken the part of Romeo among the amateurs of Antigua and always travelled

150

ABOVE: Dramatic Action Illustrated or Hamlet's Advice to Players, *dedicated to 'The Celebrated Amateur of Fashion'. He was also known as 'Diamond' Coates, 'Curricle' Coates, 'The Philanthropic Amateur' and 'The Gifted Amateur'.*

BELOW: The Gay Lothario. *Lothario is the hero of Thomas Rowe's tragedy, 'The Fair Penitent', in which Coates made his London début. The fashionable but unpopular Baron de Géramb was at the first performance and his presence caused an uproar which Coates tried to quell by offering to reimburse the dissidents if they would leave. A critic commented, 'Mr Cockadoodle Coates was eminently ridiculous as ever, which is saying a great deal'.*

with the dress of that character among his other garments. Little knowing what he was starting, he suggested to Coates that he should approach the manager of the Bath theatre with a view to giving a public rendition of the part for those not able to be present at York House during breakfast. To this Coates readily agreed. But he apparently received a rebuff, for he returned from the manager's office in a fury, declaring that he had been insulted 'and putting himself in an offensive attitude, thrust at the baize door with his cane, to the astonishments of the waiters and the terror of an old gentleman sitting in the corner with a newspaper'.

Pryse Gordon himself came to the rescue. He engaged the theatre for 9 February, 1810, professional actors were booked to play the supporting roles, a suitable charitable excuse was found and the pit was thoughtfully planted with 'a score of abigails and butlers who with a large party in the lower boxes received Romeo on his appearance with three distinct peals of applause'.

Poor Coates; he little deserved such acclaim. Throughout his six or seven years of public performances, few could be found to defend his talents. His voice, it is reported, was peculiarly harsh; every movement betrayed a total ignorance of dramatic gesticulation and, as for his stance on stage, his silk stockings and diamond knee-buckles covered 'a pair of legs jealously maintained in a position before the spectator the most favourable to the display of their symmetry'.

By Coates' later standards this first appearance went reasonably well. There were some 'ill-bred interruptions', but Romeo dealt with them firmly by crossing his arms and glaring at the offending party with great scorn and contempt. The piece actually survived into the fifth act, when the sight of Romeo grasping a crowbar to break into Juliet's tomb was too much for the audience. Amidst an uproar of helpless laughter and offers of technical advice, the curtain was rung down.

Unknowingly, Coates' first English audience had deprived itself of what was to become famous as one of the masterpieces of his histrionic technique: his death scene. He would dust the stage with a handkerchief, spread the handkerchief out carefully, place his expensive hat on it and then deign finally to succumb. On at least one celebrated occasion when he died, in the words of a contemporary eyewitness, 'on the body of the really unfortunate Juliet', he was so pleased to be greeted with round after round of vehement applause, that in the midst of the storm the dead Romeo solemnly rose to life, advanced towards the orchestra, wearing a highly gratified smirk and gravely placing his legs in the favourite position, bowed to his patrons. He then solemnly walked back to his post beside his poisoned mistress – in whom certain movements about the waist indicated she was far from being as dead as she appeared and deliberately, with identically

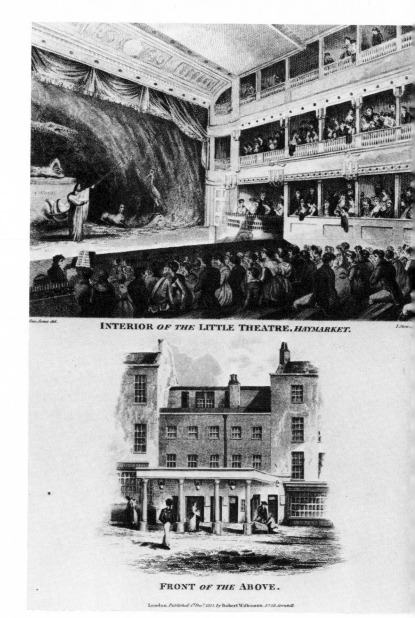

INTERIOR *OF THE* LITTLE THEATRE. *HAYMARKET.*

FRONT *OF THE* ABOVE.

London. Published 1st Dec.r 1815. by Robert Wilkinson. N.o 58. Cornhill.

LEFT: Romeo Coates as Romeo, *his most spectacular and famous role, the death scene giving him an opportunity of displaying his best histrionic technique. He would dust the stage with a handkerchief, spread the handkerchief out carefully, place his expensive hat on it, then deign finally to succumb.*

RIGHT: The Little Theatre, Haymarket, *where Coates played Lothario and where he addressed his detractors from the stage, which was to become almost part of the stock-in-trade of his acting.*

the same gestures and articulation, died again.

Coates' reputation was made at Bath, and he began a rapid progress from the provinces to the West End that would have been the envy of many professional actors. He appeared at Brighton where, it is reported, he astonished the 'acquatics and submarines of the Sussex coast'. He also appeared at Richmond and Cheltenham. There, the polished guests at a private performance showed themselves too polite to jeer, and all would have been well but for an unhappy accident. In the course of the play Romeo has an exit line, 'Oh let us hence, I stand on sudden haste'. This Romeo, however, refused to budge and, when the prompter called, 'Come off, come off Mr Coates', he replied that one of his diamond knee-buckles had gone astray and he would come off as soon as he had found it.

Meanwhile Coates took up residence in London and it was not long before the famous scallop-shaped curricle appeared among the bucks and dandies of Bond Street, its diamond-encrusted occupant enveloped in sweltering furs to shield him from a climate less balmy than that of his native land.

Soon Coates' name and nicknames were to be seen in the pages of the periodicals of the day. His arch-enemy was *The Satirist*, but it is an article in *The Scourge* of December 1811 that best conveys the theatrical style and mannerisms of 'The Amateur of Fashion'. 'In the school of Coates, dignity is denoted by strutting across the stage in strides two yards long; agony by a furious stamp of the foot at the end of every second line'. The student of Coatesian acting 'must learn to commit at least three mistakes in every line of the play' and 'to pronounce perfect "purfet", burden "barden" and memory "memarry" '.

That very month the London audiences were able to judge the accuracy of this description for themselves. On 11 December, 1811, Coates trod the boards of a London theatre for the first time.

A new theatrical prodigy was needed. Master Betty, the 'Young Roscius' from Belfast, had too long amazed it with his juvenile brilliance in the great Shakespearean parts. In 1804 Pitt had even adjourned Parliament to enable its members to see the boy wonder in *Hamlet*. But then the 'Young Roscius' had been only twelve. Now he was nearly twenty and no longer a paragon. In his place there appeared 'The Philanthropic Amateur' who, readily giving his services for charity, was to play Lothario, the noble hero of Thomas Rowe's tragedy *The Fair Penitent*, at the Haymarket. Coates, in his London début, had decided to eschew that character whose name had become associated with his own and to essay instead the work of a different playwright.

The Amateur's reputation had flown before him. Thousands were turned away disappointed from the box office while others offered up to five pounds in an attempt to get behind the scenes. Rarely can the first appearance of an actor on the London stage have been so enthusiastically anticipated.

Lothario's costume was magnificent, 'wrought in a species of silk, so woven to give it the appearance of silver' and plastered with diamonds. The audience too was glittering; it included two dukes, a bevy of earls and viscounts, the Portuguese ambassador; and the leading actor's famous friend, the Baron de Géramb.

ABOVE: The Rival Romeos or Coates and Mathews, *Charles Mathews in 'At Home', a farce in which, in the character of Romeo Rantall, he holds Coates up to ridicule. Mathews imitates Coates' habit of putting the action of the play second to the polite duty of greeting a friend in the audience – in this case Coates himself.*

BELOW: Pit, Boxes and Gallery, *a theatre audience in 1836, an etching by George Cruikshank.*

Bucks Have At Ye All, 'with Extempore additions by the Amateur Comic-Tragedian as Delivered at the Haymarket Theatre, 10 December, 1811'. Coates parried the abuse of a critical audience by reciting 'Bucks, have at ye all', as had the great Garrick on similar occasions.

The Baron was a lion of society. He had arrived in England in 1810 to discuss the recruiting of 24,000 Croatians for the British army. His moustachios were the envy of London, his sidewhiskers were copied by the Regent and his splendid uniform became the model for the dress-wear of the British hussar regiments.

Unfortunately, however, when the Baron appeared in his box at the Haymarket he was no longer universally popular. Not a single Croat had materialized, despite his vast expenses born by the British taxpayer. So great indeed was the outcry when he arrived at the theatre, that the play had to be delayed by half an hour. Then, when at last Lothario came out, with more bravado than sense, he bowed to the Baron's box. The chorus of cock-crows was deafening. In vain the hero stepped forward halfway through the play and offered to reimburse from his own pocket those who were causing the commotion, if only they would leave. Somehow the piece managed to struggle to its fourth act, but there the curtain fell. Again the audience was denied one of Coates' glorious stage deaths.

The critics were almost universally hostile, *The Satirist*, for instance, remarking that 'Mr Cockadoodle Coates was eminently ridiculous as ever, which is saying a great deal'. So vicious indeed were the critics of the daily newspapers that Coates was stung to reply with a letter to the *Morning Herald*. In it he demonstrates a dignity that rarely appeared among his actions on stage.

His willingness, manifested that previous night, to address his detractors from the stage (a right Coates clearly felt to be one of the privileges of his amateur status) became almost part of the stock-in-trade of his acting. In truth, he often showed a fine spirit in these counter-attacks and sometimes he would even recite the monologue 'Bucks, have at ye all', which the great Garrick had been known to use on similar occasions.
This includes the splendid lines:

> Ye bucks of the boxes who roar and reel,
> Too drunk to listen and too proud to feel.

With these words Coates would point ferociously at whatever box he felt had most mercilessly heckled him.

In 1811 Romeo fell in love. The object of his affections was a society beauty, Miss Tilney Long of Wanstead, a very fashionable lady indeed, who numbered among her other admirers the Duke of Clarence (later William IV) and the Baron de Géramb himself. Against this powerful opposition the amorous thespian resorted to poetry and showered the lady with odes which he had had ingeniously written for him by, among others, Boswell's daughter Euphemia. Despite such appeals as 'Give me your hand – your cash let others take', Coates' passion fell

Letter written by Romeo Coates to Charles Mathews *dated 25 February, 1813, on hearing that he was to be ridiculed in 'At Home'. 'Now Sir, Tho' I may act singularly on some occasions, it is my determination not to suffer myself to be the laughing Stock of every person who chooses to ape my manner. Therefore if you dare to imitate me in any one way this Evening I shall expect you to answer it to me in another place'*

on deaf ears and, in any case, was quickly cut short by the lady's marrying some-one else – in May 1812 – though not before Cruickshank had produced a double-page illustration for *The Scourge* showing her retreating into old maidhood horrified by the preposterous attentions of her several wooers.

There were to be many more appearances in the next few years. Often the other actors, terrified by the threatening behaviour of the audience, would get their lines confused, thus adding to the glee of their tormentors. One such mistake so offended Coates that he virtually challenged the culprit to a duel. After fifteen minutes, however, he allowed himself to be persuaded by his friends in the stage boxes, accepted an apology, shook hands before the house and continued his part. On another occasion the audience drove his Juliet hysterical and she clung to the scenery refusing to move. In the same production the corpse of Tybalt was struck sharply on the nose by an orange, at which the actor, true to the spirit of his Romeo, promptly resurrected himself and departed from the scene.

The most unfair blow Romeo's enemies were to deal him was Theodore Hook's cruel prank of February 1813, when he sent Coates a false invitation to one of the Regent's balls at Carlton House. This was the seal of fashionable approval. Coates' disappointment and humiliation at being publicly turned away must have been bitter indeed, and the decorum with which he behaved is greatly to his credit. Happily the Regent himself was furious when he heard of the occur-rence and personally sent him an invitation to come next day and view the decora-tions which were still intact.

That February also saw Charles Mathews' celebrated impersonation of him as Romeo Rantall at Drury Lane. *The Satirist* berated the famous comedian for his bad taste, but the object of the parody took it in good part. He even attended a performance, and Mathews interrupted the play to come over and shake his hand. This friendly gesture was somewhat double-edged, however, since both Lothario and Romeo were also in the habit of putting the action of the play second to their polite duty of greeting any of Mr Coates' friends who happened to be witnessing their tragedies.

The last performance was to be in 1816 at Bath. He was at last weary of being baited, and the troubles in the Indies that year were to cause the steady decline in Coates' fortunes that was to necessitate his withdrawal from fashionable life.

He outlived his enemies: Hook predeceased him by seven years, publicly disgraced for embezzling 62,000 dollars from the Mauritius treasury; *The Scourge* and *The Satirist* were both long defunct. Only his friend the Baron de Géramb survived him – by a month. Thrown out of England, under the Aliens Act, he

An Amateur of Fashion *in a familiarly absurd stance. He was in total ignorance of dramatic gesticulation, and his legs were 'jealously maintained in a position before the spectator the most favourable to the display of their symmetry'.*

had, after further adventures, finally entered a Trappist monastery in fulfilment of a vow. He died, the Abbot and Procurator-General of his order, in March 1848.

But it is surely best to leave Romeo before he became mere Robert Coates, Esq. In 1814, at the height of his powers, he actually played his famous role in the author's home-town of Stratford – and of course visited the sights. Happily Charles Mathews was also in the town. In a private letter to his wife he describes the reaction of 'Darling Fancy's child of nature' when confronted by the birth-place of the man who had caused him so much tribulation. 'There go, I cannot have witnesses, I shall cry – Ah so – eh! What? The Divine Billy was born here eh! The Pride of Nature has been in this room! I must kneel. Leave me! I don't like people to see me cry.' He also tells how previously Coates added his own inscrip-tion to the others scribbled about the Bard's bust in Stratford parish church:

> His name in ambient air still floats
> And is adored by Robert Coates.
> Few loved ones have treated their adorer more harshly.